Young**W**

POETRY COM

CW00705854

# GREAT MINDS

Your World...Your Future...YOUR WORDS

## From Hampshire &
## The Isle Of Wight

Edited by Lynsey Hawkins

 Young**Writers**

First published in Great Britain in 2005 by:
Young Writers
Remus House
Coltsfoot Drive
Peterborough
PE2 9JX
Telephone: 01733 890066
Website: www.youngwriters.co.uk

SB ISBN 1 84460 697 X

# Foreword

This year, the Young Writers' 'Great Minds' competition proudly presents a showcase of the best poetic talent selected from over 40,000 up-and-coming writers nationwide.

Young Writers was established in 1991 to promote the reading and writing of poetry within schools and to the youth of today. Our books nurture and inspire confidence in the ability of young writers and provide a snapshot of poems written in schools and at home by budding poets of the future.

The thought, effort, imagination and hard work put into each poem impressed us all and the task of selecting poems was a difficult but nevertheless enjoyable experience.

We hope you are as pleased as we are with the final selection and that you and your family continue to be entertained with *Great Minds From Hampshire & The Isle Of Wight* for many years to come.

# Contents

Natasha Bosley  (12)                                    67
David Johnson  (11)                                     68
Stevie-Liane Lili Funnell  (13)                         68
Scott Reid  (12)                                        69
Daniel Hobson  (13)                                     69
Rosie Neale  (11)                                       70
Hannah Beecroft  (13)                                   70
Bethan Ball  (11)                                       71
Hannah Townsend  (12)                                   71
Cecilia K King  (11)                                    72
Sammi-Jo Hill  (11)                                     72
Chloe Donovan  (12)                                     73
Chloe Kirkham  (11)                                     73
Bethany Cook  (11)                                      74
Kelly Herbert  (12)                                     74
Emily Woodhead  (11)                                    75
Aimee Llewellyn  (14)                                   75
Natalie Leach  (12)                                     76
Melissa Green  (11)                                     77
Stacey McNally  (11)                                    78
Bradley Alland  (11)                                    79
Kathryn Porter  (12)                                    80
Heather Charles  (13)                                   81
Elisha Weson  (11)                                      82

## Meoncross School
Sam Busby  (12)                                         83
Georgia Guest  (12)                                     84
Mitchell Clarke  (12)                                   85
Maisie Kelly  (12)                                      86
Simon Chillcott  (12)                                   87
Alex Bishop  (12)                                       87
Richard Bullett  (12)                                   88
Lucy Foote  (12)                                        88
Georgie Pick  (12)                                      89
Gilbert Cross  (13)                                     89
Melissa Bailey  (12)                                    90
Anthony Sims  (12)                                      90
Samantha Hoffman  (12)                                  91
Jessica Budnyj  (12)                                    91
Ryan McCann  (12)                                       92

## Moyles Court School

| | |
|---|---:|
| Samantha Buck  (11) | 92 |
| Steven Lucas  (13) | 93 |
| Sarah Dickinson  (12) | 93 |
| Kirsty Osborne  (13) | 94 |
| Emma Chapman-Burnett  (12) | 94 |
| Sapphire Sax  (11) | 95 |
| Olivia Annet-Short  (12) | 95 |
| Dalton North  (12) | 96 |
| Joseph Drew  (13) | 96 |
| Ryan Saunders  (13) | 97 |
| Jenny Smith  (13) | 97 |
| James Smith  (13) | 98 |
| Mali Griffiths  (13) | 99 |
| Giles Watson  (13) | 100 |
| Gemma Fraser  (13) | 101 |
| George Soan  (13) | 102 |
| Robert Fraser  (11) | 102 |
| Grace Sheppard  (13) | 103 |
| Alexander Haigh  (11) | 103 |
| Anna Peachey  (11) | 104 |
| Henry Bowen  (10) | 104 |
| Matthew Haynes  (13) | 105 |
| Michelle Long  (13) | 105 |
| Jake Harris  (12) | 106 |
| Thomas Welch  (12) | 106 |
| Matthew Head  (11) | 107 |
| Shaunie Huzzey  (12) | 107 |

## Regents Park Girls' School

| | |
|---|---:|
| Katie Roath  (13) | 108 |
| Balvinder Sidhu  (13) | 108 |
| Charlotte Eckett  (13) | 109 |
| Kirsten Tarrant  (13) | 109 |
| Megan Robinson  (13) | 110 |
| Katie Muddiman  (13) | 110 |
| Emily Street  (12) | 111 |
| Harriet Wiley  (13) | 111 |
| Penny Topley-Watts  (12) | 111 |
| Grace Mwakisunga  (11) | 112 |
| Louise Spicer  (11) | 112 |

Elliot Thompson  (12)                              157
Lizzy Lovegrove  (11)                              158
Katherine Dixey  (11)                              159

## St Anne's Convent School for Girls, Southampton
Alice Owen  (13)                                   159
Jayne Stephens  (12)                               160
Lucy Payne  (12)                                   161
Briony Horner  (11)                                162
Rachel Guyer  (12)                                 163

## Swanmore Middle School
Max Sampson  (13)                                  163
Warren Henley-Hunter  (12)                         164
Scott Benson  (12)                                 164
Jak Downing  (12)                                  165
Tara Hayward  (12)                                 165
Sadie McLean  (12)                                 166
Josh Goddard  (12)                                 166
Christie Smith  (12)                               167
Rachael Wade  (12)                                 167
Bryony Morey  (13)                                 168
Chloe Shelford  (12)                               168
Stacy van Meerkerk  (12)                           169

## The Bourne Community College
Cathryn Jordan  (11)                               169
Charlotte Thomas  (11)                             170
Eleanor Heaton  (11)                               171
Tom Portsmouth  (12)                               172
Jasmin Jackson  (12)                               172
Owen Tomsett  (12)                                 172
Ryan Hillier  (11)                                 173
Luke Edwards  (11)                                 173
Bradley Lock  (11)                                 173
Courtney Brannigan  (11)                           174
Nicole Stubbs  (11)                                174
Stacie Biggs  (12)                                 175
Peter Rogers  (11)                                 176
Ellie Williams  (11)                               176
Harriet Weetman  (11)                              177

## The Sholing Technology College

| | |
|---|---|
| Zoey Coyne  (12) | 197 |
| Hannah Bowler  (12) | 197 |
| Emma Wright  (12) | 198 |
| Tanya Harris  (12) | 198 |
| Abbey Gordon  (14) | 199 |
| Jo James  (12) | 199 |
| Alannah Knowles  (11) | 200 |
| Claire Medcalf  (12) | 200 |
| Helen Wilcox  (13) | 201 |
| Gemma Dashwood  (13) | 201 |
| Rebecca Grogan  (12) | 201 |
| Elisha Mason  (12) | 202 |
| Aimee Vine  (12) | 202 |
| Danielle Lebbern  (12) | 203 |
| Sophie Hayter  (12) | 203 |
| Louisa Osborn  (14) | 204 |
| Alice McNamara  (11) | 204 |
| Hayley Wells  (13) | 205 |
| Catherine Williams  (12) | 205 |
| Alana Steblecki  (13) | 206 |
| Paige Hunt  (11) | 206 |
| Yasmin Down  (12) | 207 |
| Ellie Thomas  (14) | 207 |
| Sorrel Patrick  (12) | 208 |
| Catherine Cove  (11) | 208 |
| Erin Strange  (11) | 209 |
| Lily Fitzgerald  (11) | 209 |
| Emily Bunney  (11) | 210 |
| Nikki Simpson  (11) | 210 |
| Samantha Mountford  (13) | 210 |
| Charlotte Parker  (13) | 211 |
| Sadie Partridge  (12) | 211 |
| Rachel James  (13) | 212 |
| Betsy-Ellen King  (11) | 212 |
| Kirby Anderson  (13) | 213 |
| Gemma Isaacs  (12) | 213 |
| Sian Edwards  (12) | 214 |
| Tina Bartlett  (14) | 214 |
| Louisa Cooper  (12) | 215 |
| Sophie Broyd  (12) | 215 |
| Ellen Brawley  (13) | 216 |
| Corinne Seymour  (12) | 217 |

# The Poems

# My Friend's Pets

Izzy has an iguana,
Marissa has a mouse,
Rachael has a rabbit,
Liam has a louse.

Paul has a puppy,
Katy has kittens,
Matt has a monkey
Who likes to wear his mittens!

Sally has a snake,
Fred has a frog,
Lyn has a lion,
David has a dog.

These are my friends
And their different pets,
But they all have something similar,
They all hate vets!

**Claire Thompson (11)**
**Bay House School**


# Football

F lying down the pitch
O ff goes the player
O utrageous fouling
T ackling their opponents
B oots too tight
A rguing with the ref
L ucky goal
L osing your temper.

**Bethany Dalton (11)**
**Bay House School**

# A Cat's Life

A cat's life is easy.
Throughout the day they sleep,
They have no school to attend,
They're enough to make you weep.

A cat's life is easy,
Everyone thinks they're cute,
They're cuddled and they're stroked,
While the dog is considered a brute.

A cat's life is easy,
They're given their food every day,
They're always warm and comfy,
That's a cat's life, I say!

**Ashley Taylor  (11)**
**Bay House School**


# Tiger Haiku

Tigers are so fast
They're mostly coloured orange
They roar like a beast.

**Amy Preston  (12)**
**Bay House School**


# The Dragon Haiku

Dragons are scary
They are also make-believe
Scary, scary beasts.

**Tara Farmery  (12)**
**Bay House School**

# Burgers, Chips And Greasy Food

I like burgers and chip shop chips,
A greasy layer sticks to my lips.
A ketchup moustache, a cheesy grin,
Surely this is a sin.

'Eat your veggies up, they're yum,
They'll make you big and strong,' says Mum.
'No way! Burgers and chips for me,
Oh can't you see?'

Burgers are heavenly, chips are dreamy,
I love to eat them hot and steamy.
I say no to veggies whatsoever,
And yes to chips and burgers forever!

**Katherine Forrester (12)**
**Bay House School**


# I Wish I Was A Doughnut

I wish I was a doughnut
So I'd get munched on every day.
The apple jam or chocolate filling
Changes the taste in a very subtle way.

**Abbey Rosam (11)**
**Bay House School**


# Crisps Haiku

Crunchy, salty snacks
They are made from potato,
They are very nice.

**Scott Arnold (12)**
**Bay House School**

# Puppies And Dogs, Kittens And Cats

P uppies are sweet
U ntidy to me
P uppies nibble on your shoes
P uppies dribble on your floor
Y ummy food to buy

D ancing together on the street
O rdinary people have them
G uess what?
S o nice to see!

K ittens are boisterous
I nto everything
T ickle their tummies
T ickle their toes
E ars are fluffy
N oses are wet
S pecial every day

C ats are sweet
A mazing to see
T reat them nicely
S itting on my lap with me.

**Emily Booth  (11)**
**Bay House School**


# Karate

K icks knocking people out
A raken to the head
R ay to pay respect
A red belt gets away lightly
T he seniors get it hard
E nds at 10th dan black belt.

**Jonathon Tugwell  (12)**
**Bay House School**

# Footy Is My Passion

Footy is my passion,
I give it my all,
The true romance in my life
Is 11 men and a ball.

I love to play footy,
And when I play footy,
I do amazing skills
And score amazing goals.

Footy is my passion,
I give it my all,
The true romance in my life
Is 11 men and a ball.

I think footy is amazing,
That's why I give it my best.
Usually I don't get a rest,
Because I'm simply the best.

**Tom Snell  (11)**
**Bay House School**

# Food

Food is good, it grows underground.
While it's growing, you don't hear a sound.

Fruit grows on tall, strong trees.
The leaves blow gently in the breeze.

Food needs rain to make it grow,
Then it's time for us to sow.

Food makes us grow big and strong,
We need food to help us along.

**Sam Gow  (11)**
**Bay House School**

# The Boy Next Door

I was walking down my street one day,
Past my neighbours' house, who'd moved away.
The new family were coming from Frome,
They were arriving here this afternoon.

When the clock struck 2pm they arrived,
Mum, Dad, a boy and a baby that cried.
He looked at me with a cheeky grin,
I glanced back and realised I fancied him.

With his golden locks and chocolate eyes,
He looked like a prince amongst the guys.
I fancied him, but did he fancy me?
I couldn't wait to see!

I went round to his house later that day,
Where we both didn't know what to say.
He smiled his cheeky grin,
So *I kissed him!*

**Catherine Lea  (12)**
**Bay House School**


# What Is Our National Food?

What is our national food?
Is it a full English breakfast,
Or a soft Yorkshire pudding?
A bag of liquorice and Dairy Milk,
Or a bowl of strawberries and cream?
Is our national food bacon and eggs,
Or is it bubble and squeak?
Is it toad-in-the-hole,
Or steak and chips?
No,
I think our national food may just be
Ye ole fish and soggy chips.

**Rebecca Clarke  (12)**
**Bay House School**

# Cold War 2004

As the human opened the door:

The carrot regiment boiled forward,
The tomatoes countered their move.
Cutlery tanks mashed potatoes,
Deserters ate their last pudding.

Peas ricocheted off the walls,
Electric openers opened the barracks,
Super-beans attacked the rear.
The microwave tortured, mutilated spies.
Bruce Pea, as hard as a frozen nut,
Launched the mouldy banana.

Silence.
Destruction left only slight traces of war,
It covered the bags of peas,
Vegetables were left to stew in their own juices,
Fruits crumbled along with cowardly custard,
As the human opened the door.

**Charles Henry  (12)**
**Bay House School**


# Milk

From the seeds with the water
To the grass to the cow
Through the stomachs
To the udders
From the udders to the milking machines
To the pasteurizers to the carton
From the carton to your mouth
Through your tea when you are slurping it
Into your bladder
From your bladder to the toilet
And then to water again.

**Ryan Duffy  (11)**
**Bay House School**

# Zero To Zero

A teenage boy has a thought,
With ideas he is fraught,
Dreams of stardom are inflamed,
But obscurity is his bane.

His next rushed thought is, *how?*
He cannot sail on a bough.
He can't read music or a clef,
So he decides to be a chef.

Escargots from France, cornflour from Maine,
Fish 'n' chips from ol' Blighty and hot chilli from Spain.
With his skill and his energy,
He's plucked out to fame.

Commercials and shows, mansions and hotels,
But one false move and from stardom he fell.
Back to frying in restaurants,
Back to the rat race and Hell.

**Matthew Twells (12)**
**Bay House School**


# Let Me Give You A Kiwi

Let me give you a kiwi,
A tough outside,
Skin as brown as a tree,
As round as a football,
As delicious as any cake,
That everyone would want to eat.

Let me give you a kiwi,
A delicious inside,
As juicy as a melon,
As green as grass,
A skin like a coat,
Covered with hair like a brush.

**Joshua Lewis (11)**
**Bay House School**

# A Fruit Bowl Of Poetry

A banana, the moon,
Its golden skin shining out,
Guiding the cherry stars,
Lighting up the round fruit bowl Earth.

A pineapple, its leaves
The jazzy feathers of a parrot's tail.
The skin of a sunset elephant,
Its soft, sweet centre, the tropical sun.

A coconut, its bristly hairs
The whiskers of a sea lion,
Its shell as hard as any crab.
So insignificant in a tidal wave of harmony.

A raspberry, its seeds
The eyes of a hawk watching you,
Its leaves, the feathers of an olive sparrow,
Its stalk, the legs of a baby robin.

The strawberry, the colour of
A glowing robin's breast at dawn in winter,
The sweet, juicy tastes of the joys of summer,
The texture of crisp autumn leaves
And the sound of a silent spring morning.

**Katie Norris  (12)**
**Bay House School**


# Spongy Muffin

Muffins come in different flavours,
Chocolate, white and even orange;
They crumble in your mouth
Like a mini landslide,
Then they go all mushy
And turn into a swamp.

**Dan Cushing  (12)**
**Bay House School**

# Cooked In Two Hours, Eaten In Two Minutes

Maroon mince wriggles like worms as I fry it on the gas stove.
The heat of the sun pounding hard on the fields
Gave me vermilion sun-dried tomatoes.
The tomato puree is red blood toothpaste.

Its neutral colour puts people off,
Or sometimes it's the slimy, greasy texture,
But in go the mushrooms all new and old.
It's not original, but it adds to taste - God bless Oxo.
The tang of the spices and herbs is mixed together
To create the most wonderful sensation.
You either love it or hate it, yes, in goes the Marmite,
A teaspoon or two to add more flavour that fizzes to your brain.
A touch of red wine for the alcohol type,
But mostly just to liven up the atmosphere.
As an extra tongue-tizzler, good old Worcester sauce,
The rich, bronze, watery substance holds a secret yet to be found.
Ah, at last we have the pasta, as yellow as the morning sun,
And becomes stringy as it boils in the pan.

I lay the table with a violent red table cloth,
Dark crimson plates and silver polished cutlery.
Set out the glasses and fresh filtered water.
Now it's time to serve up.
First I lay the pasta on the plates, pour on slowly the meat.
Then over to the table, down it goes.
'Dinner's ready,' I shout.
A stampede of feet thunder down the stairs.
Then we say grace.

It is scoffed and swallowed in less than two minutes.
So all that hard work for a few good mouthfuls of food.
For what? The love that can only be beaten by food.

**Lorna-Jane Layland  (12)**
**Bay House School**

# The Fruit Bowl

This bowl of mystery like a lucky dip at Christmas,
What will I find inside this dark cave?
First of all I feel a round, shiny surface,
It's green like a traffic light saying *go!*
Next are a pair of identical twins, red and juicy as a vampire's lips.
They look soft, but they are right hard nuts on the inside.
Now what is this? It feels like a big man's hand
But yet it's yellow as a sunflower petal
And skin like a leather handbag.
Bubbles in a bath, children in school,
The next type of fruit is like a school of children.
They come in all shapes and sizes,
These few are a right bunch.
Now in Jamaica, ladies wear these
And make a little dance with it on their head,
But to be me it's a basket with a branch breaking through the top.
Now here's another fruit that comes in all sizes,
But this time like a spotty teenager,
With the little seeds all over the surface so ruby.

**Amaryllis Hutchinson  (13)**
**Bay House School**


# Puddings

P ies are delicious, apple and blackberry, all crusty and sweet.
U pside down cake with pineapple and syrup.
D ark chocolate sponge pudding, sticky and sweet.
D elicious milk puddings, my favourite is rice.
I ce creams of all flavours, vanilla, chocolate and strawberry.
N othing can beat Pavlova and cream.
G reat British pudding, apple crumble with custard.
S orbet, sharp citrus lemon and zesty orange.

**Philip Stiff  (12)**
**Bay House School**

# Fast Food And Healthy Food

F reshly cooked burger and chips
A nd going round the corner for a Chinese
S pending time cooking these fatty foods
T ake time to think what it is doing to you

F resh pizza and chicken nuggets
O range fizzy drinks do the same
O ranges and apples are chucked in the bin
D elicious it may be but you will regret it eventually

H ave you had your fruit and veg?
E veryone needs five portions a day
A pples and plums, carrots and peas
L ooking endlessly at these healthy foods
T omatoes and onions go in a stew
H ave you missed all your fast food?

F rying's not good, just give that a miss,
O ranges and peaches are eaten in a flash
O range fizzy drinks go flat and un-drunk
D elicious burger and chips sound good now, don't you think?

**Laura Scarborough (12)**
**Bay House School**


# Spuds

The potato lay dormant under the greasy soil for a lifetime
Until the frail, crippled human killed off the extraordinary race
of the potato,
Then it got flung into a chrome pot of blistering, boiling water.
Being sizzled for half an hour, its skin started to flake like
A frustrated snake in its skin-shedding season.
Its tender, burnt skin hit the rough, chipped edge
Of the one-eyed hunchback's plate.
Then the deadly weapon pierced it with anger,
Swiftly it was put into the wrinkle-gummed man's cool mouth,
Then it was coated in sticky saliva.

**John Field (12)**
**Bay House School**

# Takeaways

Tasty chips covered in grease,
Gorgeous fish splattered with fat,
Spicy hot wings flying away,
Popcorn chicken popping away.
Big kebabs smeared with spice,
Hot and stingy, it burns the mouth.

Lovely Chinese, big and bad,
Making us bigger by the day.
Soon we will be massively obese,
Unable to move, so big and fat.
We should have eaten our veggies
While we had the chance,
And done more sports,
Like hockey, football and baseball.

Now we move to the healthy foods,
Like apples, bananas and grapes,
That never see the light of day
Because more and more want food galore,
Covered with fat, high in calories, tasty but sinful.
People eating double, storing trouble,
Becoming bigger instead of thinner.

**Nicholas Cope (12)**
**Bay House School**

# Apples

A pples are healthy
P roud and green
P retty and bright
L uscious and nutritious
E nergy giving
S mooth, juicy apples.

**Melissa O'Brien (13)**
**Bay House School**

# Bananas

Their curved shape and delicate touch,
Their sunshine-yellow skin hides their exotic personality.
Their warming taste
And cooling mind,
Bananas are the best!

Starting off life on a tree,
Then growing green, it's great!
As they get older they tend to fade
And turn a funny yellow.
Bananas are the best!

As their life turns another *crook*
When their skin starts to stain,
We know bananas have been through a lot
And we hope to see them again!

**Zoe Robson  (12)**
**Bay House School**


# Pasta

Pasta comes in all shapes and sizes,
Some are spirals and some are shells.
Some are big and some are small,
There are so many, I can't remember them all!

Pop on a pan of boiling hot water,
Then add your pasta for a taste you've been waiting for.
Pretty plain tasting food first time round,
But add some cheese and mmm . . . you're in love.

You can slurp it as loud as a straw in a milkshake,
You can smother it in sauce like lava from a volcano,
You can do whatever you want with it really,
Because whatever you do, pasta tastes good.

**Nicholas O'Rourke  (12)**
**Bay House School**

# Chocolate Cake

We sit down to dinner
All ready to consume,
Mum puts the food on the table,
The dog comes to our feet.
We feed most to the dog,
We're ready to get more.

In she comes with the food.
Our mouths water with excitement,
We wait for what seems like a century,
But now it's here, the chocolate cake.
We eat for our lives.
We left half the luscious feast.

We get sent off to bed.
I wake in the night,
My stomach tingles.
I sneak down the stairs
And into the kitchen
Looking for a treat.
I find the chocolate cake,
I take out a blade,
I think, *just a small slice.*

But no, I can't help it.
I eat and eat
Till no more is left.
I sneak back to my room.

The next day I wake up,
Soon it's lunch
And what do I find?
A slice of chocolate cake!

**Adam Mainwaring  (12)**
**Bay House School**

# Strawberries

You can taste it in the summer
in ice cream and smoothies
yoghurts and milkshakes
it's red and fantastic.

When it's in smoothies, yoghurts and ice cream
it's pink like weakened blood
and it smells so delicious.

Cherries, plums and apples
are different to strawberries
they are in all different kinds of sizes
and I just love strawberries.

Strawberries are healthy
I could eat them all day
they smell so amazing
that I want to start growing them.

Some are juicy and some are not
but whatever, I love them all
ripe ones and not ripe ones
I just love eating them.

**Nothando Dube  (12)**
**Bay House School**


# Fruit

Ah, fruit.
Their juice is as sweet as chocolate,
Their seeds nourish the ground's soil,
The seeds form to make mighty fruit trees,
Then the humans come
And the war begins.
No matter how we try, they get us,
Using knives to cut us from Mother Earth
And then we come to our end.

**Thomas Cairns  (12)**
**Bay House School**

# What The Pupil Said To The English Teacher

*(Inspired by 'What The Teacher Said When Asked What Er We 'Avin*
*For Geography Miss?' by John Agard)*

I'm sorry, Miss, I've had enough,
Of poems, books and English stuff.

Today I'd rather be in bed,
Fast asleep, looking dead.

Today I couldn't care if I got nought out of ten
In my spelling test.

Instead, today I want to do some craft,
Making beautiful crafty cards.

Alright Miss, see you later,
If you want me I'll be sitting on Mars eating chocolate bars.

Be sitting on Mars eating chocolate bars.

**Hannah Wakelin  (11)**
**Bay House School**


# The Cook Book

Maybe, just maybe, if I add this
The monstrosity of a cake mixture
That's in my dish
Will feel more like cake,
And will taste a little sweeter,
Will smell more like chocolate
And look a little neater.

Oh no! Oh bother! That's just made it runny!
It's slipping through my fingers,
Now this is not funny.
It's ruined, it's a mess, I'm a rubbish cook,
Why did I buy this expensive cook book?
It doesn't help, it just makes me blue,
And now I have the washing up to do!

**Elizabeth Beasley  (12)**
**Bay House School**

# Fruit Poem

Orange, orange, big and fat,
Hard to peel and that is that.

Bananas, bananas, tall and thin,
They also have horrid skin.

Lime, lime, nice to drink,
Sliced in lemonade it doesn't sink.

Melon, melon, as big as a football,
But don't play with it in the hall.

Grapes, grapes, nice in a bunch,
Take the seeds out, they won't munch.

Strawberries, strawberries, nice with cream,
All through summer that's my dream.

Pineapples, pineapples, chunks and rings,
But be careful of the prickly things.

Apples, apples, rosy and green,
If you polish them, they will have a nice gleam.

**Damon Jones  (10)**
**Bay House School**


# Ice Cream

I ce cream is like an icicle,
C reamy, lovely and thick,
E at it, scoff it, shove it down.

C oldness within the lick,
R eady, steady, go, go, go!
E at it fast and you'll blow, blow, blow!
A ching comes from the head,
M adness comes, and you'll be dead!

**Paul Wilkinson  (11)**
**Bay House School**

# Garlic

I give you a garlic,
It has a peculiar smell,
The smell of an onion . . .
Gone off and sour.

I give you a garlic,
Its layers as smooth as silk,
And its tracing paper skin.

I give you a garlic,
As flaky as fish food,
Or burnt skin.

I give you a garlic,
It has a bottom like a flower . . .
Or maybe as spiky as a moustache . . .
Or like a newborn kitten,
All fluffy but stood on end.

**Kristie Rees (11)**
**Bay House School**


# A Poem Of Food

Cherries are snazzy, pink and juicy,
Chips sizzle in your mouth,
Cakes are really sweet,
They're yummy in your tummy,
Cookies are full of chocolate
Which melts upon your tongue,
Carrots are good for your rabbit,
And help you see in the dark,
Custard is creamy and golden,
And warms from inside out!

**Charli Taylor (11)**
**Bay House School**

# The Mushroom

I close my eyes and see before me,
A cloud as silky as a swan's feather,
I am filled with curiosity,
As to what it could be.
Inside I see something as prickly as heather.

Then something that looks like a broccoli stem,
The top is shaped just like a dome,
Fragile as a flower.
The colour of this object gradually getting darker.

I give you a mushroom,
Flat but at the same time, round,
A fairy in legend has been known to use this as shelter.
Originally grown in the ground,
Now I'm beginning to swelter.

My curiosity turning to knowledge,
It's a mini nuclear explosion,
A light bulb,
Just sitting there,
Smiling.

**Saffron Harcombe  (11)**
**Bay House School**


# Fruit

Peaches are so fuzzy,
Apricots so soft,
Oranges have pips in,
And grapes are nice and thin.

Plums so small and round,
Bananas, long and yellow,
Strawberries, red and sweet,
And there are lots of other fruits to eat.

**Laura Potts  (11)**
**Bay House School**

# Beowulf: Dragonslayer

*(Inspired by 'Beowulf: Dragonslayer' by Rosemary Sutcliff)*

Beowulf laid down, as though to rest,
Although his sword was still clamped to his chest.
At midnight exactly, Grendel came in,
Tearing one soldier limb from limb.
The monster went for another, then more,
Blood now spattering the hall walls and floor.
His green cat-like eyes then came to rest,
On none other than Beowulf, trying his best,
To look quite asleep, his eyes were closed tight,
But still he was ready for the upcoming fight.
Grendel reared, ready to strike,
Suddenly, Beowulf's eyes came alight.
He dodged the first blow, then two more,
And then, feeling dread, the dragonslayer saw:
All the remains of his sword-brothers and mates,
Would Beowulf also share that horrible fate?
He struggled and fought against the beast,
Grabbed on the arm, Grendel forgot about his feast,
He forgot about the fight, forgot about the bout,
With a spine-chilling shriek, he finally sped out;
Into the night, but that came at a price,
His arm was still trapped in the hand like a vice.
The victims were avenged and Ecgtheow's son,
Sobbed with exhaustion, though the battle was won.

**Antony Lusmore  (11)**
**Bay House School**

# Banana

B ananas are so silly, sliding out of their skin
A nd they are so refreshingly tasty
N ever straight, always curved
A nd I always have a munch on a bunch
N o wonder the monkeys swing from tree to tree
A nd I will always eat those, lovely yellow bananas.

**Max Pointon  (11)**
**Bay House School**

# Lemon

I give to you
a lemon so sharp
a dagger couldn't compare
as yellow as a daffodil
like the sun caught forever in a photo.

I give you this lemon
because I compare it to our friendship.
They are the same in a way,
a lemon can be as sour as sherbet
like our friendship,
but through everything
the lemon's taste is as endless as numbers
just like our friendship.

So I give you this lemon
as sharp as a dagger,
as yellow as a daffodil,
as sour as sherbet,
and its taste as endless as numbers . . .
to remind you of our friendship
(and of a lemon)
always!

**Georgina James  (11)**
**Bay House School**


# Chocolate

Chocolate, chocolate, it's in my head.
Chocolate, chocolate, it's in my bed.
All day long I think *chocolate, chocolate.*
All night long I dream chocolate, chocolate.

It's creamy, it's sweet, it's delicious,
It's soft, it's squidgy, it's so tasty that I drop.
I eat it, I eat it, until I pop.
I think it, I dream it, I need to get it out of my head,
I need a good ten hours in my bed!

**Mark Lee  (11)**
**Bay House School**

# I Give You . . . Banana

I give you . . . banana!
His skin is an expensive, silky texture,
He is a chameleon, forever changing colour, from
Green . . . to
Yellow . . . to,
Yellow (with brown blodges) . . . to
Brown . . . to
Black!

I give you . . . banana!
He is hard and stern on the outside . . . but
Soft and mushy on the inside.
He is exotic, like a coconut on a tropical island,
But yet popular and well-known like a celebrity,
He is long and pointy like a knife gleaming in the sun,
His top is a minute tree-stump,
He is a long, thin rake.

I give you . . . banana!
He comes in a litter like a kitten,
But is separated later on,
His layers of hope are peeled off,
And then he screams,
Then vanishes for evermore!

**James Farmer (11)**
**Bay House School**


# Bramley

When you get a Bramley
Out of the dull, orange bag,
The shiny skin blinds you like the sun.
As you sink your teeth into the soft filling,
The juice seeps out like lava from a volcano.
When it slides down your throat with a tingle,
The taste is thirst quenching!

**Sam Wheeler (12)**
**Bay House School**

# Sweets

Sweets in a wrapper
Sweets in a jar
Sweets in a box
But you will never go far!

Sweets in a sauce
Sweets in a tart
Sweets in a bag
But you will never stop when you start!

Into the corner shop
All jars in a row
All different shapes and sizes
You will never know where to go!

Red ones, blue ones, pink ones too
Round ones, square ones, all for you
Minty, fruity, fizzy too
It's like a shop just for you!

**Bianca Cleaver  (12)**
**Bay House School**


# Chocolate

Chocolate is soft and silky,
As smooth as can be,
Crunchy Dairy Milk,
All for me.

It's bumpy, lumpy,
Doesn't make you grumpy.
It's such a treat
To have something sweet.

Some prefer white,
Some prefer plain,
But as for me,
I like it all the same.

**Joe Holman  (11)**
**Bay House School**

# What The Pupil Said To The English Teacher

*(Inspired by 'What The Teacher Said When Asked What Er We 'Avin For Geography Miss?' by John Agard)*

I'm sorry Miss I've had enough,
Of poems, books and English stuff.
Today I'd rather fall asleep,
Then do some work in the heat.

Today I couldn't care if
The whole wide world became a myth.

Instead today I'd rather run,
And play football. Want to come?

All right Miss, see you later,
If you want me I'll be on the equator,
On the equator,
On the equator,
On the equator.

**Brett Wakefield (12)**
**Bay House School**


# Poetry Day

Not a gallon of blood.
I give you a garlic.
Its skin is like the silver moon
In the darkness of the night!

It will blind your big eyes,
Fill you with hurt.
It's a promised light
In this darkness.
Its fierce attack will
Stay with you
Forever!

It will take away the evil
In your heart!

**Natalie Fuller (12)**
**Bay House School**

# Taste

I like parsley sauce on fish,
I like beef with horseradish,
Tasty spaghetti Bolognese,
Don't forget the tuna and mayonnaise.
I like potato chips,
With Mexican flavour dips.

Fresh, succulent, tasty pork,
Open the bubbly, take out the cork.
On Sundays I like a roast,
On Mondays I like beans on toast.

Carrots, peas, asparagus and rice,
Put together with a pinch of spice.
Baked potato with cheese,
'More, Mum, please.'

Roasted, fried, fresh and battered,
Over the floor vomit is splattered.

**Kalem Walton (12)**
**Bay House School**


# What The Pupil Said To Miss!

*(Inspired by 'What The Teacher Said When Asked What Er We 'Avin For Geography Miss?' by John Agard)*

I'm sorry Miss, I've had enough,
Of poems, books and English stuff.

Today I'd play on my PS2,
Well, anything's better than listening to you.

Today I couldn't care if you started biting,
It still wouldn't be as boring as writing.

Instead, today I want to skive,
And shove your head down a beehive.

Alright Miss, I'll see you later,
If you want me I'll be glued to a game of Space Raiders.

**Connor Jezard (11)**
**Bay House School**

# The Vampire's Garlic

I give you a garlic,
It looks like an unopened flower,
But in the eyes of a vampire
It is deadly like a black widow spider.
The look of it does not frighten the vampire,
But the smell of it does.

I throw the garlic at the vampire,
The vampire recoils in disgust,
As the stench assails his senses,
He is like a worm struggling from the ground.
As he tries to escape I get my stake,
And I drive it through his stone-cold heart.

He burns in flames of relief,
As he is free from the vampire curse.

**Chloe Wood  (13) & Rebecca Wise  (12)**
**Bay House School**


# Garlic

I give you a garlic, to you from me,
It is pale white for you to see.
If you draw near, it will singe your skin,
The ruthless murders will no longer begin.

It will send you to the depths of Hell below,
Where there, vampires will cease to grow.
Far from it, they will burn to ash,
Just like demons put to a match.

Its juice is strong, with a deadly stench,
So stay back you beast, or I will strike,
Because I'm not scared, I just dislike.

I give you garlic, with pain and might,
Because it is lethal with you in its sight.

**Jude Coates  (12)**
**Bay House School**

# Roast Dinners

Carrots, broccoli and cauliflower,
The amazing smell of steamed veggies,
Then come the golden brown Yorkshire puds, all sat in perfect rows,
Right behind, looking the best, come the crispy, fat, thin, big, small
Crunchy or floppy roast spuds which gleam in the sun,
Or have crispy black spots which look as dark as a black hole.
Then we have the best, but hardest bit about the roast dinner,
The choice of meat is pretty hard. The tasty chicken,
Mouth-watering lamb, beastie beef, gleaming turkey or pork and ham!
I'm sure you all have a favourite, and you eat it proud with no sound,
You think it's all over and the food is fine,
Until the thick, brown, yummy, rich gravy comes.
You either love or hate gravy, but if you love it you're in for a treat.
Your roast dinner goes from fine to excellent,
That's pretty neat!

**Dan Eldred  (13)**
**Bay House School**


# Grendel's Here!

*(Inspired by 'Beowulf: Dragonslayer' by Rosemary Sutcliff)*

As Grendel moved over the moors,
To cast more havoc in town,
He cast his mighty shadow on all the shrubbery around,
Grendel was a lion's roar,
Waiting to be heard,
He wasn't in to apple pies, pears or lemon curd,
Grendel was a meat eater,
He could rip you to shreds,
And you better watch out 'cause he's ripped off a few heads,
He came into the mighty Hereot,
While people slept in sweat,
But Beowulf was in the main hall,
Waiting to be met.

**Jamie Cutts  (11)**
**Bay House School**

# The Plight Of Grendel

*(Inspired by 'Beowulf: Dragonslayer' by Rosemary Sutcliff)*

Bounding through the night he came,
Seeking the scent of blood,
Through the bars that blocked his way.

Triumphant he stood,
Swooped down for the kill,
Took out his prey with all his skill.

Greedily he went for the next,
But his arm was grabbed just then,
And torn under the grip of thirty men.

He screamed and cried,
For he had come to great harm,
He cursed the man who took his arm.

Then Beowulf rejoiced,
As Grendel took flight,
For he had destroyed,
This creature of the night.

**Tim Squirrell (11)**
**Bay House School**


# What The Pupil Said To The English Teacher

*(Inspired by 'What The Teacher Said When Asked What Er We 'Avin*
*For Geography Miss?' by John Agard)*

I'm sorry Miss, I've had enough
Of poems, books and English stuff
Today I want to see my aunt and ride on a tortoise plant
Today I couldn't care if I won a million pounds
Because I'd be too happy if my sister left town
Instead today I think I will . . . roam around town
Or go to Canada with my pants down
All right Miss, see you later, if you need me you will have to wait
Because right now I'm going to be late.

**Jessica James (11)**
**Bay House School**

# I Give You A Pineapple

I give you a pineapple
With the love of my heart
So juicy and sweet
But where do I start?

Shaped like a face
Green stalks like cool hair
All prickly and bumpy
And inside it's all bare.

Juice as sweet as honey
All orange and bright
Inside it's soft as a bunny
Oh pineapple you have such an amazing sight!

Grown in hot countries
Then sent over here
People put so much work into this
Oh give them a cheer!

Pineapples so yummy
Pineapples so sweet
The skin is not eaten
But inside it's a treat.

I give you this pineapple
With the love of my heart
So juicy and sweet
The stalk like a dart!

**Laura Eke  (11)**
**Bay House School**


# Dolphins Haiku

Dolphins - they are wild,
They do tricks to impress you,
But not extinct yet.

**Charlotte Fisher  (12)**
**Bay House School**

# Garlic!

I give you a garlic
A rainbow of colours
Brown, white, pink and green
White snowflakes
Flaking off like dandruff.

I give you a garlic
An elephant's trunk
But no noise comes out of that trumpety trunk
Look at the bottom
What do you see?
A beautiful flower pretty as me!

I give you a garlic
A moustache of hairs
A Hallowe'en pumpkin
Smiling
But there's no face.

I give you a garlic
A wonderful garlic
With magical powers to dry your tears
Which will stay with you throughout the years.

So here is your garlic
Of it, please take care
Keep it forever
If you eat it
*Beware.*

**Alice Gordon  (11)**
**Bay House School**


# My Favourite Food Haiku

Food is great and nice,
Like pizza, chicken, rice, mmm.
The best will be chips.

**Liam Wilmshurst  (12)**
**Bay House School**

# Garlic Poem

I give you a garlic,
It is my own,
I got it from far away, where it was grown,
Its smell and fragrance is rather strong,
For like an onion its smell lasts long,
Its flaky skin peels with hardly a touch,
Like sunburnt skin and pastry and such,
Its stem is as stout as a rake,
And its stubbly bottom like a beard but fake,
Its inside cloves as hard as a rock,
But its taste when cooked is nothing to mock,
And its shape, a ballet dancer in a pink frock,
So now you'll agree,
That garlic, you see,
Is the best vegetable there ever could be!

**Harry Williams  (11)**
**Bay House School**


# Garlic Poem

I have a strong odour and pungent taste
and if you eat me you may screw up your face

The bottom of me is like a small flower
and the flavour I give off is full of power

I'm made up of cloves but not what you wear
I'm used to scare vampires so just beware

My colour is as creamy as milk but don't drink me
I'm as small as a golf ball but don't put me on the tee

I have segments like an orange but not as sweet
I peel away like an onion and can be sprinkled on your meat

I give you a guess, smell my breath, what have I been eating?
Garlic!

**Jasmine Bernice  (11)**
**Bay House School**

# What The Pupil Said To The English Teacher

*(Inspired by 'What The Teacher Said When Asked What Er We 'Avin For Geography Miss?' by John Agard)*

I'm sorry Miss I've had enough of
Poems, books and English stuff.
Today I'd rather go to space
Instead of staying in this dull place
Today I'd like to reach up high
And ride a cloud in the sky
All right Miss, see you later
If you want me I'll be in America enjoying the sun.
I'll be in America enjoying the sun!

**Paige Cowdrey (11)**
**Bay House School**


# Beowulf Poem

*(Inspired by 'Beowulf: Dragonslayer' by Rosemary Sutcliff)*

B eowulf, big and really strong,
E veryone knew he could do no wrong,
O wing his life to the king,
W olf man he felt was under his wing,
U naware of what lay ahead,
L ooking to repay the king for his bed,
F inally for Beowulf he slayed the monster's head.

**Toby Cooperthwaite (11)**
**Bay House School**


# Beowulf Vs Grendel

Grendel smashed and Beowulf grabbed
Grendel howled and Beowulf pulled
Grendel fought and Beowulf tightened
Beowulf held and Grendel stumbled
Beowulf yanked and Grendel screeched
Beowulf held and Grendel ran with one arm.

**Dan Lawrence (11)**
**Bay House School**

# Beowulf

*(Inspired by the story 'Beowulf: Dragonslayer' by Rosemary Sutcliff)*

Beowulf lay still,
Planning to kill the monster,
Plaguing Hereot hall.

A green flame in eyes,
Grendel destroyed the great locks,
Smelling flesh and blood.

A crash awoke them,
Though they were never asleep,
Beowulf ready.

Grabbing Grendel's wrist,
Grip with the strength of thirty,
Grendel's wrist breaking.

All power in hand,
Beowulf gripped the monster,
Helping Hereot hall.

There was one option,
But would cost very dearly,
The only way left.

Beowulf smiling,
Thinking he was triumphant,
Grendel breaking free.

Grendel's arm torn off,
He screeched whilst running away,
The grip not broken.

**Alexander Durkan  (11)**
**Bay House School**

# Grendel Goes!

*(Inspired by 'Beowulf: Dragonslayer' by Rosemary Sutcliff)*

Grendel, the man-wolf
A beast with no heart.
When his cold, green, fiery eyes glare at you,
It feels like you're being stabbed by a dart.

Grendel crept up to the barred mead hall doors,
A fresh smell lingered in the air. Humans!
Despising humans,
Grendel snarled with rage!

He smashed through the doors
Screaming with fury!
He hated humans, every single one.
Grendel's emerald eyes flickered slightly.

Why? Why, a feast lay waiting for him!
Every man was sleeping! All except one.
Grendel grabbed a man,
Shoved him in his mouth.

Yum! That was tasty
Now for a few more.
He gripped another tightly with his claw,
But the strength of 30 men gripped back quick!

Beowulf, our hero, clung on fiercely,
He didn't lose a fight to anyone.
Grendel howled with pain,
This wasn't the plan!

Grendel thrashed about!
Beowulf gripped tight!
Could they be fighting like this all night?
No! Cos Beowulf pulled even harder.

Grendel's limbs were ripped apart, he ran of sobbing, fast as a dart.
And that, my friends, is how Beowulf, Dragonslayer,
Saved Herrot the Hart!

**Lauren Howard (11)**
**Bay House School**

# Beowulf: Dragonslayer - A Poem

*(Inspired by 'Beowulf: Dragonslayer' by Rosemary Sutcliff)*

Beowulf was a powerful man,
With the strength of thirty men in the palm of one hand,
With chain mail and a sword, such wonderful things,
He can afford to do a favour for the very old king.

Grendel was fierce, such a terrible thing,
But Beowulf ripped his arm off limb by limb,
Grendel ran away, scared and afraid,
Never to come back to that mead hall again.

'Hooray,' Beowulf cried with tears of joy,
'I've scared Grendel away forever, oh boy!
ˉ For celebrations,
I shall, I shall,
Drink in that mead hall with my dearest pal.'

**Laura Smith  (11)**
**Bay House School**


# What I Think About English

*(Inspired by 'What The Teacher Said When Asked What Er We 'Avin
For Geography Miss?' by John Agard)*

I'm sorry Miss, I've had enough
Of poems, books and English stuff

Today I want to jump around
I don't want to be quiet, I want to make a sound

Today I couldn't care if my grammar was wrong
Or if my poem had turned into a song

Instead, today, I could be
At home all snug and watching TV

If you want me
I will be sailing on the big blue sea
Sailing on the big blue sea.

**Eloise Ritchie  (11)**
**Bay House School**

# English, I've Had Enough

*(Inspired by 'What The Teacher Said When Asked What Er We 'Avin For Geography Miss?' by John Agard)*

I'm sorry Miss, I've had enough,
This boring English is so tough.
Today I want to drink some Coke,
Watch TV or read a joke.
I couldn't care less about spellings or dictionaries,
I'd like a cup of tea if you please.
I'd like to snuggle up in bed,
Not read poems instead.
So who cares less of your books and English stuff?
So if you want me I will be in bed
Because as I said
I've had enough,
I've had enough,
I've had enough.

**Reem Scott (11)**
**Bay House School**


# Grendel Vs Beowulf Poem

*(Inspired by 'Beowulf: Dragonslayer' by Rosemary Sutcliff)*

Grendel snuck in to steal
His very easy midnight meal
But Beowulf was ready for this attack
For when Grendel walks in he'll give him a whack!
Grendel thought this like grabbing a hen
But he did not expect the strength of 30 men.
Grendel tried to get away
But this was a toll he had to pay.
Beowulf was ripping the tissue of him
Oh how could Grendel be so dim?
Grendel broke free in the end
But there was one thing he had to mend.
His arm had been lost to one of the men
So Grendel ran off back to his den.

**Oliver Troise (11)**
**Bay House School**

# Beowulf The Legend

*(Inspired by 'Beowulf: Dragonslayer' by Rosemary Sutcliff)*

The hall was engulfed
In silence and stillness,
Grendel crept down
From his seaside mess.
He ripped his way
Through the doors,
The men awoke
Ready for war.

The stench that filled their nostrils;
The sight that entered their eyes;
Was horrific!

With swords brandished
The men approached,
Beowulf stepped forward
With confidence,
Grabbed hold
Of the monster's arm,
Ripped it off
But still was calm.

The monster had been defeated,
Celebrations filled the hall!

**Helena Cochran  (11)**
**Bay House School**


# What The Pupil Asked The English Teacher

*(Inspired by 'What The Teacher Said When Asked What Er We 'Avin For Geography Miss?' by John Agard)*

Sorry Miss, I've had enough of poems, books and English stuff.
Today I'd rather watch TV. I thought that was plain to see.
Today I couldn't care if Sam turned into a pot of strawberry jam.

Instead, today I want to play, have you got that, OK?

All right Miss, see ya later
If you want me I'll be in Ireland examining a crater.

**Patrick Heathcote  (12)**
**Bay House School**

# Grendel's Attack!

*(Inspired by 'Beowulf: Dragonslayer' by Rosemary Sutcliff)*

Grendel, the night-stalker, sniffed around us,
He smelt the sweet blood of the brave warriors,
Grendel crept into the room silently,
A stench seeped around us.

When Grendel walked into the pitch-black room,
He sent a chill down my spine whilst walking fiercely,
He was about to pick a warrior,
The youngest of all the warriors was killed.

Grendel was going to his next victim,
When suddenly Beowulf leapt into action,
He grabbed the creature's arm very violently,
The creature screamed with pain.

Beowulf had the strength of thirty men,
Grendel was terrified as his arm was ripped from his side,
Grendel ran off into the night screaming,
Beowulf saved Hereot Hall with glory.

**Jordan Nicholas (11)**
**Bay House School**


# The Fight

*(Inspired by 'Beowulf: Dragonslayer' by Rosemary Sutcliff)*

Beowulf lay awaiting the return of the
Mighty Grendel.
Beowulf,
With his sword brothers,
Were here to end it all.

The footsteps came without a sound,
Until Beowulf and his brave men found,
The ugly beast with no loving heart,
Who could be dead within one dart.

The fight began and all was won,
With Beowulf alive,
And Grendel done.

**Yasmin Ashfield (11)**
**Bay House School**

# The Brave Beowulf

*(Inspired by 'Beowulf: Dragonslayer' by Rosemary Sutcliff)*

There is a wise warrior called Beowulf
Beowulf comes in search of the gruesome Grendel
So Beowulf comes with fierce, frightening, pumped-up muscles.
He shuffles through the lush green grass to the hall of Hereot.
The squeaky door is open!
It is all silent.
Beowulf looks around.
His fellow blood brothers are gone!
He sniffs the air.
A clue is found!

Beowulf follows the smell and blood like a bloodhound.
He follows the sea salt smell until it has gone.
He comes to a cold, damp, dirty, deep sea inlet.
Beowulf timidly walks in.

**Kirsty Kinnaird  (11)**
**Bay House School**


# What The Pupil Said To The English Teacher

*(Inspired by 'What The Teacher Said When Asked What Er We 'Avin*
*For Geography Miss?' by John Agard)*

I'm sorry Miss, I've had enough,
Of poems, books and English stuff.
Today I want to play outside,
Cos English I just can't abide.
Today I couldn't even care less,
Even if we got to make a mess.
Instead I want to have great fun,
In the sea and in the sun.
Alright Miss, see you later,
If you want me you'll have to wait,
See you later, Miss, I won't come back.
I'll be in McDonald's eating a Big Mac,
I'll be in McDonald's eating a Big Mac!

**Ashleigh Wright  (12)**
**Bay House School**

# Food Poem

Pineapples are green like a tropical sea,
They're golden yellow and sweet as can be.
Their skin is rough and spiky to touch,
But the fruit is juicy and I love it so much.
It tastes so sharp, it tastes so sweet,
It really is quite strange to eat,
It makes you dribble all down your chin.
You can even buy it in a tin.
You use your fingers to pick it up,
The juice will have to go in a cup.
You can eat it in a bowl or with cheese on a stick,
It's your decision, you must pick.
This fruit really is by far the best,
If I were you, I'd forget the rest!

**Kate Paterson  (12)**
**Bay House School**


# Grendel, We've Had Enough!

*(Inspired by 'Beowulf: Dragonslayer' by Rosemary Sutcliff)*

I'm sorry Grendel, we've had enough
Of you killing our sword brothers and stuff
When you come at dead of night
When there's not even a speck of light
You creep up on us
Just like a particle of dust
Listen Grendel, you don't understand
My brothers and I own this land
I, Beowulf, have the strength of thirty men
So why can't you just stay in your den
With your little, weedy dam
Don't forget we own this land!
We own this land!

**Gemma West  (11)**
**Bay House School**

# Beowulf Beats Beast

*(Inspired by 'Beowulf: Dragonslayer' by Rosemary Sutcliff)*

Grendel came bounding in
Hungry for some dinner,
Little did he know
His days were getting thinner.

Beowulf beat the beast
Tore him limb from limb,
Grendel ran off screaming
And made it a real big thing.

Hrothgar was really happy,
He was now a pleasant chappie,
Beowulf got ready to go home,
Thinking his work was done.

Grendel's Mum came up,
And gave them all a shock,
Beowulf got ready for battle,
Again,
Again.

**Jackson Todd  (11)**
**Bay House School**


# Garlic

It is flaky as sunburnt skin,
But pricks like a sharp pin.
To look at it you would not think
It could let off such an awful stink.
In your mouth it tastes like heaven,
When it also comes from Devon.
Parsley they say is the saviour,
To rid you of that awful flavour.
When you mix it with your meat,
Ooh it does taste so sweet.
If you can't get parsley in a hurry,
Just try and buy a Murray!

**Trey Hutchings  (11)**
**Bay House School**

# In Came The Battlers

*(Inspired by 'Beowulf: Dragonslayer' by Rosemary Sutcliff)*

In came the battlers,
Snarl, rip, tear,
In came the almighty battlers,
In came Grendel,
He's urging for death,
Craving for death.

In came the crusaders,
Snarl, rip, tear,
There's blood on the wall,
The blood of the almighty crusaders.

In came the king's men,
Into the battle,
Now he was outnumbered,
By one single man.

Off goes his arm,
Off goes Grendel, screeching in pain,
He's overpowered by one single man,
*Beowulf.*

**Stuart Bailey (11)**
**Bay House School**


# Stood In The Dinner Queue

Stood in the dinner queue,
Thinking how good I'll be:
Steamy vegetables,
Chicken and peas,
My mum will be pleased!
But then out of the corner of my eye I spy,
Hot, thick, crispy chips,
And though I try I can't resist!
'Did you say broccoli?'
'No, sorry Miss, I meant *chips!'*

**Nicola Taylor (12)**
**John Hanson School**

# Food A, B, C

A pples, so crunchy, cold and fresh.
B ananas, smooth and yellow.
C orn, crunchy and so yellow.
D oughnuts, soft and sugary.
E ggs, smelly, runny, yummy.
F ish, yummy but sometimes smelly.
G rapes, smooth and green as the grass.
H ot sauce on your yummy food.
I ce cream as cold as winter.
J am, all runny and yummy.
K iwi, green and juicy.
L emons, all yellow and sour.
M ushrooms, all shapes and sizes.
N uts, all crunchy and yummy.
O nions, all crunchy, horrible and make you cry.
P eas, all green and round.
Q uick as cooking curry.
R adish sauce all over your food.
S ausages, all tasty and long.
T omatoes, all red and round.
U ncooked carrots are really crunchy.
V odka, as nice as food.
W edges, as nice as normal chips.
eX tra sauce all over your chips.
Y ummy yoghurts for pudding.
Z ingy salt all over your chips.

**Matthew Humphreys (12)**
John Hanson School

# Cinquain

Korma
Tastes good with rice
Yellow, smooth and tasty
Oh how it is nice without spice
Lovely.

**Paul Szekeres (11)**
John Hanson School

# My ABC Favourites

A is for Arsenal, the best football team ever!
B is for Bianca, my sister's name
C is for Cyprus where I used to live
D is for drumming, another of my hobbies
E is for egg which I like on toast
F is for football, one of my favourite sports
G is for Greg, that's *me!*
H is for home, that's where I live
I is for ice cream which is very cold
J is for Jackson, my second name
K is for Kerrang! my favourite music channel
L is for listening and learning
M is for Martin, my dad's name
N is for naughty, which I sometimes am
O is for orange, my favourite fruit
P is for pork, my favourite meat
Q is for Quavers, I pack them in my lunch box
R is for red, my favourite colour
S is for sweets which I enjoy very much
T is for Teresa, my mum's name
U is for my school uniform
V is for Vans, my favourite skating shoes
W is for wine which I have on Christmas Day
X is for X-ray, which I had done on my fractured wrist
Y is for yellow, my sister's favourite colour
Z is for zebra, you will see it at the zoo.

**Gregory Jackson  (11)**
**John Hanson School**


# Haiku . . .

I love chewing gum,
Blowing bubbles with a bang!
*Splat!* over my face!

**Emma-Louise East  (13)**
**John Hanson School**

# Christmas Belly

Into the cauldron goes,
A jug of fresh hippo's toes,
A pinch of salt,
And a hedgehog scraped from the road.

A fat pig's belly,
Some ogre's eye jelly,
A sprinkle of pepper,
And owl's droppings (still smelly).

Entrails of dog,
Toad's warts from a bog,
A dash of vinegar,
And tail of a dog.

This does make,
Without mistake,
A cure for Christmas bellyache!

**Danielle Dunsdon  (11)**
**John Hanson School**


# My Best Things

My perfume's fresh scent,
The last day of Lent,
Watching TV,
As free as can be,
Dark chocolate is better,
Than receiving a letter,
Ljungberg is the best,
Better than the rest,
Usher is great,
Nothing better than winning a debate,
Heat of the summer sun,
Warm cinnamon bun,
Strawberries and cream,
And finally, no one that is mean.

**Melissa Jeffery  (12)**
**John Hanson School**

# The Alphabet Poem

A is for apples, a crunchy thing to eat,
B is for balloons, which you have at your birthday,
C is for Curtis, and that is my name,
D is for dinner, I like nice foods,
E is for elephants, they are big mammals,
F is for Florida, a warm, cosy country,
G is for gorilla, they swing in the trees,
H is for horses, they gallop through fields,
 I is for igloo, they're small and cold,
J is for jungle, they are nice and green,
K is for kitten, a baby cat,
L is for Lauren, that's the name of my friend,
M is for Monopoly, a good game to play,
N is for Nile, a big river in Egypt,
O is for opticians, where you get your glasses,
P is for purple, a nice colour,
Q is for questions, something everyone asks a day,
R is for rhino, a fierce animal in the wild,
S is for spider, a nice creature to have,
T is for tiger, a very fast animal,
U is for umbrella, something to keep you dry,
V is for vets, where you take your pets,
W is for water, a healthy thing to drink,
X is for X-ray, where you see your bones,
Y is for yellow, a bright colour,
Z is for zoo, a cool place to be.

**Curtis O'Connor  (11)**
John Hanson School

# Cinquain

Soft bite
delicious red
taste flowing as I bite
soft meat melting in my mouth, yum
love it!

**Jade Mills  (13)**
John Hanson School

# What I Like!

I love eating chocolate and sweets,
And getting lots of little treats.
Horse riding shows are a lot of fun,
Especially when you have just won.
Watching films at the cinema with my mates,
You never know what surprise awaits.
Watching 'Friends' on a Friday night,
With a big packet of crisps, I'm alright.
My favourite song is 'A Thousand Miles',
When I sing it everyone smiles.
Christmas is the best time of the year,
Everybody's happy, it's a great atmosphere.
Lots of presents, the Christmas tree,
And going on a big shopping spree.
Holidays are cool in the sun,
Water-skiing and sunbathing are great fun.
But the best thing is being with the people I love,
And doing all of the above!

**Lily Jackson (12)**
**John Hanson School**


# My List Poem

I love lots of things . . .
Chocolate, boys and Saturday mornings
Boyfriends, clothes, shoes and money
Cherry Drops, photos and friends that are funny
I like the colour pink and my phone
I talk to my friends when I am alone
I like my room and my bed
It's a place to rest my head
From a long day at school
Learning things that don't make sense at all!

**Xavia Byrnell (12)**
**John Hanson School**

# The Cauldron

Into the bubbling cauldron goes . . .
A unicorn's horn,
Eye of newt,
And really cheesy goblins' toes.

Tail of rat,
Stinkbug's eggs,
And leftover ogre's dregs.

Tongue of dog,
Tarantula's head,
And a lizard I think is dead.

And one more thing,
That must go in,
A poisoned fin.

To give to my maid,
That I haven't paid . . .
'Would you like to try my soup dear?'
*Ah, ha, ha, ha . . .*

**Sammi-Jo Hill (12)**
**John Hanson School**


# Strawberries

We love all the seeds,
We love strawberries,
We are so easy to please,
Dipped in cream,
Makes me scream,
I love strawberries in cream.

Strawberries freshly picked,
Cream out of the fridge,
Both mixed together,
Is lovely forever.

**Joe Foster (12)**
**John Hanson School**

# My Favourite Fruits

These are some of my favourite fruits
Melon, orange, mango and pear.
They are all so sweet and juicy
You feel like eating them all day long.

They are good and healthy
And help you with everyday things.
Because they give you energy
So you can run and swim.

They are all different shapes and sizes
Their tastes can be strange and new
Sometimes they are sweet and juicy
And sometimes they're bitter too!

So that's why we should eat fruit
Because it's good for you.
There are all different choices
So you can choose the one you like too!

**Riya Patel  (12)**
**John Hanson School**


# My Fruit Poem

Fruits here, fruits there, fruits, fruits everywhere
Banana, apple, kiwi, pear, fruits, fruits everywhere
Oranges, oranges, oh so round
In orange peel they'll always be found
Coconuts, coconuts bump you on the head
Although I'd rather have scrummy coconut juice instead
Grapes, grapes, some call them fruit fakes
Because wine makes you giddy and your head ache
Blueberries, blueberries are in the famous Roald Dahl book and movie
And Violet goes home looking rather fruity
Fruits here, fruits there, fruits, fruits everywhere
Banana, apple, kiwi, pear, fruits, fruits everywhere!

**Chloe Mills  (12)**
**John Hanson School**

# Curing Hunger

Put into one large pot
Some polished pig and
Some slime and grot
A tail of rat and
A tarantula's leg
Ogre's blood,
Dragon's drool,
Hocus pocus,
Do your deed,
Toil and trouble,
Boil and bubble,
Until it's broth.
Are you ready?
Entrailed spell,
What will happen if I smell?

**Hannah Bolsover (12)**
**John Hanson School**


# Wheat And Meat

I walked up the apples and pears,
I was totally unaware,
As I fell over my slabs of meat,
Then I saw some bees and honey,
I thought I can hi-fi some wheat and meat,
From the hop and pop,
And I can take my china plate,
I hawked out of my mouse,
I saw my china plate,
We walked down the toad in the hole,
She said, 'Have you got bees and honey?'
'Yeah, it's right here,
In my Lucy Locket's tummy!'

**Abigail Baldwin (13)**
**John Hanson School**

# Food Poem

A pple - crunchy, fresh and juicy
B utter - tasty, delicious and golden
C hocolate - creamy, milky and rich
D uck - cruel, disgusting
E gg - fried, scrambled and poached
F ish - fingers, chips and battered
G rapefruit - sharp and sour
H am - bad, good and fatty
 I ce cream - creamy, cold and yummy
J am - sugary, fruity
K iwi - tasteless, wet
L ime - sweet, sharp
M altesers - crunchy, sweet
N aughty, nice and tasty
O lives - black, tasteless
P rawns - awful, horrible
Q uiche - hot, bacon, egg
R aw pepper - sour, disgusting
S trawberries - juicy, fresh
T omato - sweet, ripe (red), yellow
U gli fruit - ugly, shapeless
V eal - juicy, young meat
W atercress - pepper, dark green
oX 's tongue - tough, chewy
 Y oghurt - creamy, fruity, chilled
 Z esty, yellow, lemon.

**Ruby Baker (12)**
**John Hanson School**

# Food Filled A To Z

A ppetising apple,
B right red beetroot,
C rispy chicken,
D elicious doughnuts,
E gg fried rice,
F ish and chips,
G reat food to try.
H ot haggis,
I ce cream and nuts,
J iggy jelly,
K orma curry,
L uscious lasagne,
M unch, munch, munch, much more to taste.
N ectarines, very juicy,
O ranges the same,
P erfect Polos,
Q uite nice quiche,
R hubarb crumble,
S ausage sandwiches,
T oo many to say.
U pside down cake,
V ery berry pudding,
W affle Belgium are my fave,
X mas dinner,
Y ummy yams,
Z abaglione, they're all my favourite foods, so now tell me yours!

**Rachel Sievewright  (12)**
**John Hanson School**

# Some Of The Things I Like And Hate

I like it when my Coke is nice and cool,
I hate it when people act like fools,
I like chocolate on strawberries,
I hate chocolate on blueberries.

I hate custard on my toast,
I hate people when they boast,
The one thing that would ever cheer me up,
Is my auntie's new dog, he's only a pup.

I hate it when my dad watches football,
I like it when my friends give me a call,
I hate it when my mum eats scones,
I like it when the opera has gone.

I hate Marmite on my bread,
Oh do I love chocolate spread,
I think now I'm going to stop,
That is all I've said, otherwise my head will pop.

**Carianne Few  (12)**
**John Hanson School**


# Foods

I like carrots but I don't like peas
Burnt toast is horrible but Marmite toast is nice
Pizza is yummy but only when it's pepperoni
All the others are not so tasty unless it's cheese
Ice cream is cool but salad cream is too sharp
I hate fish and most meats too but I'm not a vegetarian
                                because I eat chicken
I love bacon, especially when it's crunchy and crispy
I like mashed potato but not when it's in a jacket!
I like macaroni, in a tin or my mum's, but I hate pasta
                        when it's on its own.

**Michael Horne  (12)**
**John Hanson School**

# Schooldays

When I woke up this morning,
I rubbed my mince pies.
I listened to my brother frying,
As he fries and fries and fries.

I went and had a bubble and squash,
Then I ran down the apple and pears.
I grabbed some rosy lee,
And took my daily fair.

When I got to slop and gruel,
I ran to my first class.
I sat down with my fig and dates,
And waited for lemon and lime to pass.

When the munch bell rang,
I stick of chalked to the dining hall.
I bought a plate of strawberry pips,
Then I date them all.

When slop and gruel was over,
I stick of chalked home.
I sat on my apples and pears,
And listened to my mum on the dog and bone.

**Tom Clarke  (13)**
**John Hanson School**


# My Poem

I like fish fingers, beans and mash,
I like a large chocolate stash,
Apples, oranges, bananas and pears,
Give me them *now* before I go spare,
Cheese with mould makes me go cold,
Spinach is good, so I'm told,
Treacle tart and custard, it's really good,
Fill my tum with lots of pud.

**Kym Bickell  (12)**
**John Hanson School**

# Alphabet Poem

A pple cake
B lue cheese pie
C arrot cake
D ivine

E el pie
F rogs' legs stew
G oulash
H umorous and fun

I ce cream slosh
J elly and custard
K iwi fruit
L ovely to try

M oney chocolate
N achos
O range and cream
P lenty to eat

Q uark and olives
R adish with wilted salad
S alted crisps
T otally fine

U gli fruit
V odka and Coke
W alls Balls and chips
X treme good times
Y ou know these all but my favourite is a
Z inger Burger from KFC.

**Shirley Murtagh (13)**
**John Hanson School**

# The Menu!

A pple pie
B anana cake
C ool cucumber
D elightful to try

E el pie
F ried fish
G aggling goose
H orrible, I won't try this

I ncredible ice cream
J uggling jelly
K ellogg's Frosties
L ovely, I'll try these

M outh-watering mango
N aughty nuts
O range octopus
P erfect, but where's the Tango!

Q uail
R unning rice
S lippery snails
T asty (I think). Imagine a whale

U pside down cake
V ictoria sponge
W atery wine
X mas is soon, I'd rather have a swine
Y ucky yoghurt
Z apping zest

I hate this, I'd rather look after a pest.

**Sophie Arundell  (11)**
**John Hanson School**

# Food ABC

A pples are crunchy, crisp and ripe
B ananas are smooth, soft and mushy
C urry is tingy, tangy and spicy
D oughnuts are sickening, sweet and sticky
E ggs are plain, slithery and messy
F udge is soft, sugary and sweet
G rapes are juicy, sour and tasty
H ot dogs are slimy, slithery and scrumptious
I ce cream is creamy, cool and delectable
J elly is wibbly, wobbly and simply delicious
K ebabs are meaty, moist and mouth-watering
L imes are zingy, zangy and zesty
M ushrooms are dull, damp and dreadful
N ectarines are nice, nutritious and succulent
O ranges are juicy, refreshing and sharp
P eanut butter is pasty, nutty and thick
Q uiche is crumbly, cheesy and soft
R aspberries are red, rosy and moist
S ausages are fatty, filling and firm
T una is fishy, smelly and fresh
U gli is thirst-quenching, tasty and fresh
V elveet is highly flavoured and full of dairy
W atermelons are large, mouth-watering and ripe
X igua is appetising, bulky and matured
Y oghurts are runny, fruity and lively
Z est is sour, sweet and acidy.

**Natalie Power (13)**
**John Hanson School**

# Food

A pple - juicy, sweet and ripe
B urger - tasty, yummy and scrummy
C urry - spicy, filling and really nice
D oughnuts - sweet, yummy and delicious
E gg - boiled, fried and poached
F ruit - disgusting, tasteless and horrible
G rapes - sweet, sour and ripe
H ot Pot - yummy, tasty and hot
 I ce cream - cold, sweet and scrummy
J elly - wobbly, sweet and nice
K iwi - yucky, gross and disgusting
L amb - chewy, yummy and hot
M armite - scrummy, gooey and sticky
N uts - smelly, horrible and nutty
O range - sour, smelly and disgusting
P eas - smelly, grotty and green
Q uavers - cheesey and scrummy
R aspberry - smelly, not tasty and bumpy
S trawberry - hairy, sour and smelly
T omato ketchup - yummy, sour and slimy
U pside down cake - spongy, sour and yummy
V ienetta - scrummy, sweet and cold
W atermelon - horrible, sweet and round
X mas pudding - yummy and one of the best foods in the world
Y am - yucky, sour and not nice
Z abaglione - sweet, nice and yummy.

**Rebecca Walton (11)**
**John Hanson School**

# Things I Like

I have written a list about what I like,
This includes a nice long family hike,
But in a funny way,
It sort of represents my day;
Watching SpongeBob on the telly,
A warm sensation in my belly.
I also like art . . .
Well, that's a start!
Watching scary shows,
Helping people out of ultimate lows.
Snorkelling out in the blue sea,
Telling jokes that are aw-ful-ly funny.
Acting like I'm a star,
Writing stories that take me far.
Eating pizza and sweets,
I only get them as treats!
Going out in my super boat,
*Ooopps,* don't mean to gloat!
Being with my family and friends,
Then my fun never ends.
Watching Arsenal win on the telly,
With Thierry Henry giving it a great welly!
But that actually is not all,
Any more will make this poem super tall!

**Natalie Day  (14)**
**John Hanson School**


# Cinquain

Yellow
Soft-centred fruit
With rubbery, thick skin
Grow on trees and bought in bunches
Tasty.

**Joseph Attwood  (13)**
**John Hanson School**

# Alphabet Of Food

A pples are sweet, crunchy, juicy
B ananas are squelchy, gooey and soft
C urry is hot, spicy and tangy
D oughnuts are sugary, sticky and doughy
E clairs are chocolatey, sticky, sweet
F udge is sticky, gooey, brown mess
G oats' cheese is white and creamy
H aricot beans, small and beany
I ce cream is creamy, crunchy, melting cold ice
J am tarts, crunchy pastry, sweet jam
K iwi, sharp, tough, prickly skin
L amb, succulent, meaty smell
M ange tout, flat, moon-shaped pea pods
N ectarines, sweet, juicy, lovely mush inside
O ranges, tough skin, juicy centre
P ork is succulent, meaty, tough
Q uince, pear-shaped green fruits
R unner beans are alright but are quite stringy
S wede is mushy, messy, yellow goo!
T una, juicy, watery, messy, mushy
U pside down cake is upside down and back to front
V egetable soup is runny, disgusting soup
W atercress is crunchy, watery and peppery
eX tremely lovely foods and here are some more
Y oghurt is sloppy, runny and milky
Z angy, zingy, tangy, lemon sharp and zesty.

**Laura Budd  (11)**
**John Hanson School**


# Cinquain

Chocolate
sweet and sickly
richest, smoothest texture
flavour dissolving on my tongue
chocolate.

**Sophie Brown  (14)**
**John Hanson School**

# The Best Of The Best And The Worst Of The Worst

My favourite things are
sausage and mash
peppered swede
late night shopping
my purring cats
days out in London
Pudsey Bear.

Things I don't like
my mum working nights
cabbage,
Stilton cheese,
games of chess
schooldays and early mornings
jellied eels from Germany.

I like snowball fights with my brother
potatoes, any kind,
crispy bacon
long phone calls
the smell of fresh-cut cucumber
bright colours
diamond rings.

Things I don't like,
rock bands
fatty meats
dreams you can't remember
days that are too hot
mean friends that blank you out
black and white newspapers.

Here's more things I love
Christmas Day
ice-skating outdoors with my best friends
lemon torte with ice cream
Tigger
spare time
white winters
magazines
fairy lights
stars at night.

More things I don't like
meat pies
leeks, that's enough to make me cry
horror films
sad endings
sushi
eggs
boring TV shows
shoes that don't fit.

Things I like
Moulin Rouge
Titanic, the film
jelly
chocolate ice cream
chocolate bars
parties
pink fluffy things
movie stars
musicals
watermelon
these are my favourite things.

I could go on forever
and I'm sure you could too
but I have to stop there
or I'll run out of paper!

**Harriet Kirkdale (12)**
**John Hanson School**

# A - Z

A is for animals, any domestic type
B is for Barbados, the best beaches
C is for coconuts because I like the milk
D is for dogs, I've got 2 dogs
E is for elephants with long trunks
F is for football, it's the best sport in the world
G is for guinea pig, so sweet and so small
H is for hats, to stop heatstroke
I is for ice, so cold and strong
J is for JHS, so big and new
K is for kindergarten for kids to enjoy
L is for love, sweet and romantic
M is for mums, so strict and ugly
N is for nuts for squirrels to eat
O is for orange, a lovely fruit
P is for pockets, very handy
Q is for Queen - very important
R is for running, good exercise
S is for soup, so very tasty
T is for teamwork, to work together well
U is for umbrella to stop you from getting wet
V is for vase, keep pretty flowers in
W is for water so we can drink
X is for X-ray to make bones cool
Y is for yoga, good exercise!
Z is for zebra, lovely and stripy.

**Callum Sweeney (11)**
**John Hanson School**

# Food

A pples - crunchy, sweet and crispy.
B iscuits - sweet, yummy and crunchy.
C urry - tangy, spicy and hot.
D oughnuts - sweet, sticky and soft.
E gg - fried, scrambled and boiled.
F ruit - healthy, sweet and crunchy.
G rapes - fruity, watery and squishy.
H am - meaty, tasteless and terrible.
I ce cream - cold, sweet, runny and soft.
J am - horrible, sweet and sticky.
K iwi - tasteless, tangy and fruity.
L asagne - tasty, saucy and meaty.
M ango - tangy and fruity.
N uggets - meaty, crispy and delicious.
O nions - smelly, makes your eyes water.
P izza - saucy, spicy and bready.
Q uiche - soft, meaty and cheesy.
R olls - bready, crumbly and soft.
S weets - nice, sweet and chewy.
T una - horrible, fishy and bumpy.
U pside down pudding - fruity, creamy and rich.
V ery different types of food.
W atermelon - soft, juicy and yummy.
eX tremely nice foods.
Y oghurt - creamy, gloopy and liquidy.
Z abaglione - it tastes Italian.

**Laura McLean  (11)**
**John Hanson School**

# Acrostics

I like

L asagne
I guanas
K angaroos and
E lvis Presley

I don't like

D odos
O ranges
N ectarines
T omatoes

L eeks
I ce cream
K iwis or
E ggs

I love

L ittle
I guanas
K ittens and
E ggs

I hate

H ungry
A lligators and
T iny
E els.

**Jessica Tarrant (13)**
**John Hanson School**

# My Alphabet Poem

A pple crumble
B ananas all sweet
C hocolate all sticky
D oughnuts all sugary and jammy
E ggs poached
F rench fries all crispy

G arlic in bread
H oney all sticky and sweet
I ce cream's all cold and nice
J elly all wobbly on a plate
K iwi in different colours
L ollipops so colourful

M unchies all crunchy
N uts all nutty
O ranges all sweet and bitter
P ineapple chunks
Q uince, sharp and tangy
R ice pudding's sweet to eat

S trawberries in summer
T rifle with layers
U gli fruit all different and strange
V inegar, strange but nice on chips
W alnuts like nuts at Christmas
X mas pudding all sweet and nice

Y oghurt all sticky in many flavours
Z ucchini, green and sweet.

**Natasha Bosley (12)**
**John Hanson School**

# The Claw

This is the
shape of the monster's
claw, glinting on its massive
paw, which quietly opened the
bedroom door and swung up with
one terrible roar, over the bed, in the
moonlight, it stabbed
in to the sleeper to
silence his snore,
blood dripping down
on the floor when
the monster started
to gnaw, then went
back out the door.

**David Johnson (11)**
John Hanson School


# I Like . . .

I like custard and candyfloss,
I like pizza and being boss,
I like trifle, cola and friends,
But they sometimes drive me round the bend.

I like books and apple pie,
I like a lovely clear blue sky,
I like chips and rhubarb crumble,
But when you ask your mum for this she grumbles.

I like tea cakes especially with jam,
I like my sarnies with cheese and ham,
I like chocolate cake and custard,
But it's annoying when your brother puts it with mustard.

**Stevie-Liane Lili Funnell (13)**
John Hanson School

# This Really Isn't My Crème Brûlée!

I woke up in a dreadful plate
Because I bumped my loaf of bread

I trotted down the apples and pears
And tripped over my plates of meat

Bumping my loaf of bread again
This really wasn't my crème brûlée

I picked my jars of honey
And started off down the street

I think I'll go to the local shop
And buy myself the Daily Kipper

Now walking next to a man
I think I will find a master flan

I checked in my wallet . . .
I needed more jars of honey!

**Scott Reid (12)**
**John Hanson School**


# The Harbour

The warm sun crystallising the sea
The grey end of the summer day
The winds ripple against the sails giving a vibration sound
The smell of hot, lush, golden chips on a cool, breezy evening
As the sun sets, casting long shadows upon the harbour's front
The cool sea breeze whipping the smell of salty water
                              across your face
All the extraordinary shops, each with its unique items
The colourful fudge shops with sweets from liqueurs to mint to
                              desert sand to tropical fruit flavours
Each item new to common people
The grey washed water glides smoothly along as you eat
                              the warm fish.

**Daniel Hobson (13)**
**John Hanson School**

# Sunday Dinner

The roast is in the oven,
My favourite meal of all.
The kitchen hot and steamy,
With saucepans on the boil.

Soon the dinner's ready,
The table set and waiting,
Plates warming in the oven,
How much longer to wait?

Upon the plate Mum then puts
Meat and lovely gravy.
Crispy roast potatoes,
And parsnips, golden brown.
And piled high along the side,
My favourite vegetables.
Leeks and carrots, broccoli too.

And then the moment comes
When I get to eat.
It seems that in no time at all
My plate's absolutely clear!

**Rosie Neale  (11)**
John Hanson School


# Our Poem

F aith has gone,
R ights, what rights?
E veryone gone,
E verything's the same,
D isowned everything
O nly one phone call,
M ight get out.

**Hannah Beecroft  (13)**
John Hanson School

# To Cure A Bellyache

Goblin's earwax,
Sticky and runny,
All mixed round,
Into its tummy.

Eel entrails,
Manure too,
Griffin's toenails,
Smell a bit like poo.

Scale of a rainbowfish,
Horse teeth, dragon claw,
Guts and blood,
But there's still more and more.

Then boil bubble,
Toilet trouble,
Bubbling, mixing,
Boil bubble.

**Bethan Ball  (11)**
**John Hanson School**


# All About Me!

I like waking up upon a Sunday morning,
With the smell of breakfast dawning.
The taste of croissants with melted butter,
Strawberry jam, what a flutter.
I don't like to clean my teeth.
I don't like cooked beef.
I like to go and meet my nan.
I like bacon cooked on a pan.
I like playing with my mates.
I like staying up late.
And what a way to end the day
With my nan's roast dinner!

**Hannah Townsend  (12)**
**John Hanson School**

# Christmas Stomach Ache

Dragon drool
Snakes' slime
Tiger tongue
Lemon and lime

Cure this stomach ache
Of Christmas pud
Cure them well
The way they should

Donkey dung
Spider eggs
Tiger teeth
Lion legs

Round and round
The cauldron we go
Stir the pot
To and fro

Rabbit retina
Flamingo feather
Bird backbone
Hellish heather

Keep the pot
Nice and hot
And don't forget
To drink the lot!

**Cecilia K King  (11)**
**John Hanson School**


# Bonfire Night Haiku

With smoke in the air,
Watching fireworks going off
Eating marshmallows.

**Sammi-Jo Hill  (11)**
**John Hanson School**

# Dolly And Pip

I woke up one morning,
And ran down the apples and pears,

Made a cup of rosy lee,
And sat on the lilac bears,

For lunch I had some dolly and pip,
With some bed and fleas,
For tea I had some chicken flippers,
With some greens and bees,

Before I went to my cosy bed,
I had a cup of yo-yo,
I couldn't have a cup of coffee,
That was a definite no-no!

**Chloe Donovan  (12)**
**John Hanson School**


# My Food Poem!

I like veg and I like stew,
Cabbage smells, but it's good for you!

Beans, beans simmering on the hob,
Why can't I have corn on the cob?

I like carrots and I like peas,
And any fruit that grows on trees!

Apples rosy and pears ripe,
I'm so glad my mum hates tripe!

Fish 'n' chips I can smell,
Can I have some sauce as well?

**Chloe Kirkham  (11)**
**John Hanson School**

# A Cure For Christmas Tummy Aches!

First put in some slime and grot,
Now throw in some baby's snot,
Next chuck in a handful of dragon claws,
Then lob in a logful of tigers' paws!

The ear of an elephant may sound bad,
But if you add the fin of a shark, it'll make you go mad,
Now all you need is a few griffins' toenails,
But that's not all because you still need some rats' tails!

Ten teeth from a horse's mouth will do you good,
Throw in ten unicorn horns that taste of wood,
Slurp out the guts of five snails and spit them back out
into the pot,
Now it's time for extra flavour which is ogre's blood, boiling hot!

**Bethany Cook (11)**
**John Hanson School**


# Breakfast!

I woke up one morning and ran down the apples and pears,
I looked out the window with my sleepy mince pies,
To find a beautiful currant bun shining brightly in the sky,
I went to the kitchen to fetch a lie,
Or even a leg and some queens,
I finally filled an empty doll so,
Then I went back up the apple and pears to get my bow tie,
My best china plate was waiting at the gate,
I didn't want to see her so I hit out all her pork and beef.
Then she said with blood in her mouth, 'I thought you were
my date . . .'

**Kelly Herbert (12)**
**John Hanson School**

# A Wicked Witch's Wonderful Spell

A cauldron of slime and grot,
an eye of a griffin that's not,
all of that will go in a pot.

A dragon's claw,
a mouse's jaw,
that's what I asked for.

Things that are scary,
but not food that's dairy,
a wing off a little fairy.

A lizard's leg,
a toad that's in bed,
a tongue that's not fed.

A unicorn's horn that's not bit,
a monkey's hair that's not got a nit,
that's what will go in it!

**Emily Woodhead (11)**
**John Hanson School**

## Chickpeas Or Parsnips, Which One?

Chick peas
Golden yellow
Tempting, mouth-watering
Sweet, creamy, sharp, tasteless
Hardening, off-putting
Dirty, beige
Parsnips.

**Aimee Llewellyn (14)**
**John Hanson School**

# Food Poetry!

A pples, crunchy, juicy and fresh.
B read, soft, dry and baked fresh.
C risps, crunchy and salty.
D oughnuts, sticky and messy.
E ggs, fried or scrambled, still yummy.
F ries, mashy fried sticks.
G rapes, red or green but juicy.
H am, fresh and slimy, also yummy.
I ce, you will shiver because it's so cold.
J am, sticky and messy, all flavours.
K itKat, chocolatey and crunchy.
L asagne, yummy, cheesy and hot.
M ustard, horrible, yucky and spicy.
N oodles, slivery, long worms.
O ranges, juicy and wet.
P izza, cheesy and yummy.
Q uiche, chewy bacon and pastry.
R aspberries, juicy and sour.
S ausage rolls, full of pastry.
T izer, fizzy and wet lemon.
U ncooked meat with fat.
V egetables, healthy and crunchy.
W ater, wet with no flavour.
eX tra helping of custard.
Y ummy yoghurt with strawberries.
Z inging, zesty lemons.

**Natalie Leach  (12)**
**John Hanson School**

# Alphabet Poem

A is for animals which I think are the best,
B is for birds that fly around,
C is for cats that purr,
D is for dog, my favourite animal,
E is for elephant, a very big mammal,
F is for fish, which swim around,
G is for giraffe which has the longest neck,
H is for hippos, which wallow in water,
I is for ice cream that drips down the cone,
J is for jelly that wobbles,
K is for kangaroos that bounce,
L is for lilies that are very pretty flowers,
M is for monkeys which swing from trees,
N is for nans who are very special,
O is for oranges which are juicy,
P is for pandas which come from China,
Q is for Queen who is Royal,
R is for rabbits which hop,
S is for snake that slithers along,
T is for tears that pour down your face,
U is for umbrella that you use when it is raining,
V is for vase in which you hold flowers,
W is for whale that swims in the sea,
X is for X-ray which is a picture of your bones,
Y is for yellow, the best colour ever,
Z is for zebra which has black and white stripes.

**Melissa Green (11)**
**John Hanson School**

# The Alphabet Poem

A is for animals of any domestic type,
B is for the beach, the favourite place to get a tan,
C is for Christmas, my favourite time of year,
D is for my dog called Bonnie,
E is for Easter where you get loads of chocolate eggs,
F is for McFries, one of my favourite types of food,
G is for grapes, sweet and sour,
H is for happy because I like being happy,
 I is for ice, nice in drinks,
J is for jumps, star jumps and high jumps,
K is for kind because people are nice when they are kind,
L is for light because it helps us see,
M is for money 'cause I like shopping,
N is for night because I like going to sleep,
O is for orange, nice, fresh and sweet,
P is for polar bear, my favourite animal,
Q is for quit which I can't do,
R is for rides for I like funfairs,
S is for Stacey, my name,
T is for two, my lucky number,
U is for up for I wish to move up in a level,
V is for villa because I love staying in neat villas,
W is for water because it makes us clean in baths and showers,
X is for Xbox, it's very enjoyable,
Y is for yellow, the colour of summer,
Z is for zips because it closes my coat.

**Stacey McNally  (11)**
**John Hanson School**

# My Alphabet Poem

A is for animals, sea types are my favourite
B is for Benidorm, my first holiday abroad
C is for cats, I have four
D is for diving at my local pool
E is for energy, which keeps me going all day
F is for football, which I play and watch
G is for goal, I scored one
H is for holiday in the boiling sun
I is for ice, which is very slippery
J is for jumping to header a football
K is for kicking a football
L is for launching paper aeroplanes into the air
M is for munching on food
N is for nails which I like to hammer in
O is for octopus with its waving tentacles
P is for pencil for drawing with
Q is for quatre, the French word for four
R is for rabbits eating carrots
S is for Sven Goran Eriksson, the England football manager
T is for Teddy Sherringham, my favourite footballer
U is for Uranus, my favourite planet
V is for voice, so I can speak to my friends
W is for West Ham United, my favourite football team
X is for X-ray, I can see my bones
Y is for yo-yo, bouncing up and down
Z is for zebra prancing about.

**Bradley Alland  (11)**
**John Hanson School**

# Alphabet Food

A pple crunchy,
B iscuit soft,
C hocolate creamy,
D airy Milk melted,
E gg fried,
F rench fries salty,
G alaxy smooth
H ash browns tasty,
I˚ ce cream cold, are all the things I like.

J elly wobbly,
K iwi chewy,
L emon sweet,
M ince bitty,
N uts hard,
O range smelly,
P arsley horrid,
Q uince gross,
R abbit nasty, they're all the things I hate.

S ausage,
T una,
U gli fruit,
V egetables,
W atermelon,
X mas food,
Y oghurt,
Z ucchini, are all the foods that are OK.

**Kathryn Porter (12)**
**John Hanson School**

# My Mum Taught Me The ABC

A mazing apples
B eautiful bananas
C old chocolate
D elightful doughnuts
E vil eggs
F ragile fried bread
G orgeous grapes
H aunting hot dogs
I mmature ice lollies
J iggle jelly
K ind kiwi
L ather liquorice
M agic mushrooms
N ervous nits
O rdinary oatmeal
P ale pancakes
Q uiet Quavers
R adiant radishes
S imple salad
T winkle treacle
U nreliable ugli fruit
V aluable vanilla
W onderful watermelon
X tra large Xmas pud
Y esterday's yoghurt
Z ero zabaglione.

**Heather Charles  (13)**
**John Hanson School**

# Untitled

A pple - crisp, fresh and juicy
B anana - soft, subtle and mellow
C hocolate - sweet, dreamy and tasty
D oughnut - sugary and sticky
E gg - runny, poached or boiled
F udge - chocolatey, creamy and chewy
G rapes - juicy, bitesized and fresh
H am - pink, thin and wet
I ce cream - cold, meltable, raspberry ripple
J elly - wobbly, fruity and flavoured
K iwi - tangy, strong and tingly
L emon - zingy, sour and tangy
M ango - messy, juicy and vibrant
N achos - cheesy, crispy and spicy
O range - taste bud tormenting
P izza - cheesy, hot and tomatoey
Q uince - fruity and juicy
R ice - small, tasteless strips
S ausages - meaty and sizzling
T una - wet, messy, stinky
U pside down cake - delicious and luxurious
V eal - deer, white meat
W atermelon - exotic, big and juicy
X mas pudding - burning, cherry
Y olk - inside of egg - yellow
Z ingy hot sauce - hot, eye-watering.

**Elisha Weson  (11)**
**John Hanson School**

# Anakin's Asteroid Anchovies

Serves an army of R2 robots

*You will need:*
1 interplanetary destruction
3 hyperspace jumps
5 spare repair kits
4 unexplored Venusian moons

*Ingredients:*
100g Evil Sith Lord
2 Jedi Masters, diced
1 R2-D2, grated
1kg aliens
1 alien warship, pre-cooked
2 double-sided lightsabers, semi-skimmed
10kg hanger, whipped

*Method:*
Place 100g Sith Lord in 10kg hanger.
Cover in 500g aliens, mix thoroughly in warship.
Add R2-D2, armed. Use 3 repair kits.
Pre-heat 2 grated Jedi Masters at 100°c
Thoroughly stirred with lightsabers.
Add 2 repair kits to resulting battle.
Using hyperspace jumps, explore Venusian moons.
Bake in planetary destruction zone,
Remembering to baste occasionally.

**Sam Busby  (12)**
**Meoncross School**

# Fairy Cakes

Serves - 7
What you will need: Palace

*Ingredients:*
5 tablespoons of poison
100g of a little girl
Pinch of mother
1/2 a teaspoon of a dad
A drop of evil stepmother
1 spoonful of fairy godmother
1/2 a teaspoon of evil stepmother's assistant
679g of fairy
1,000 tonnes of elephant

*Method:*
Preheat the oven at gas mark 8.
Place dead mother in tray and bake for 10 minutes.
Take out dead mother and replace with dead dad.
Add in a drop of evil stepmother and stir until bubbling.
Take out pot and add 1 spoonful of fairy godmother.
Add 679g of fairy.
Stir until bubbling.
Add 1,000 tonnes of elephant and put in the oven
Until the top is light brown.

**Georgia Guest  (12)**
**Meoncross School**

# Mitch's Poisoned Pancakes

Serves 7

*You will need:*
1 village idiot
1 cave
1 pointy palace
1 dusty track

*Ingredients:*
200g of king
200g of laced queen
1 kilo of prince
1 dragon
50g of spice of witch

*Method:*
Preheat the village idiot to 500°c.
Throw in the dragon to make it hot and spicy.
Cream the king and queen together using the pointy palace.
Fold in the prince using the dusty track.
Put the mixture on the ground and flatten using the cave.
Put in the oven for 200 years,
Or until black, burnt and looks disgusting.
To decorate sprinkle spice of witch on top.
For extra zing, add 6 orangaries.

**Mitchell Clarke  (12)**
**Meoncross School**

# Maisie's Magical Moonlit Meringues

*You will need:*
A moonlit night in an enchanted forest

*Ingredients:*
1 love-struck maiden
1 lonely stable boy
1 jealous rival
A sprinkle of desire
A pinch of rose petals
A dash of romance
A cup of desperation
1 bowl of loneliness
An ounce of rage
1 tbsp of sorrow
2 tsp of tragedy
6 grams of happily ever after

*Method:*
Preheat the love of the maiden
And the stable boy in a pot full of love.
Stir in one jealous rival with a bowl of loneliness.
Mix in a cup of desperation and a sprinkle of desire.
Stir in a pinch of rose petals and a dash of romance.
Whisk in a moonlit horse ride to the forest.
Pour in an ounce of rage and stir for five minutes.
Fold in two teaspoons of tragedy and rub in an ounce of butter.
Sprinkle in one tablespoon of sorrow.
Blend all together with six grams of happily ever after.
Leave to set for two long romantic hours until soft and light.

*Note: This must be eaten on a moonlit night with the one you love.*

**Maisie Kelly (12)**
**Meoncross School**

# Football Is A Game

Football is a game,
A religion to many,
It is a matter of life and death.

The referee rules the pitch
And the eleven players on it,
With red and yellow cards.

The goalkeeper is the last line of defence,
Run fast and shoot,
And you may get a goal.

Manchester City and Real Madrid,
Are the teams to follow!
But every week I support Fareham Town.

A London derby game,
With Arsenal playing Tottenham,
In my house it's Mum versus Dad.

**Simon Chillcott  (12)**
**Meoncross School**


# Alphabet Spaghetti!

Where's my name? Where's my name?
I know it is in here somewhere!
Just the other day it was here,
But not today, it has gone, not to be seen
Every other letter is a H or G
There is my mum and dad
But not mine, it's not here, nowhere to be seen
I know it is in here somewhere
'Cause just the other day
It was right here.
I have the A, the L and the X
But I really need that E.
Oh, there it is under the Z
Look at me, I am all tomatoey
Uh oh, my mum's gonna kill me!

**Alex Bishop  (12)**
**Meoncross School**

# The Full English Breakfast

First come the cornflakes
Crisp and crunched,
Then comes the bacon
Fatty and scrunched,
Also the fried egg
Flying saucer in a cloud,
The tomato is there
Swimming in its sweet juice,
Present is the mushroom
The umbrella with taste,
Never forget sausage
Bursting with flavour,
Always the black pudding
The hater of pigs,
Toast with marmalade
The final ingredient.
What a wonderful way
To start the day.

**Richard Bullett  (12)**
**Meoncross School**


# Candyfloss

Light and sticky,
Pink and pretty,
Sweet and neat,
On a stick.

Round and round it goes,
In the machine.
Not long until they give it to me.
Can't wait until it's mine, all mine.
Nobody else can touch.
Oh no, here comes my dad,
Guess what? He has taken it,
Oh how I miss it so much!

**Lucy Foote  (12)**
**Meoncross School**

# Defoe

In the dark I sat and shivered,
Cold and wet,
As the rain lashed down,
I peered through misted eyes.
Across the grass, streamed with mud,
White markings barely visible.
People running fast and furiously,
With only one purpose in every mind.
Sound all around me,
Loud and then suddenly quiet again.

Out of the blue a shout went up,
A whistle blew,
I raised my arms,
All around me people did the same,
The noise was horrendous yet joyful,
I smiled to myself.

We'd won one-nil.

**Georgie Pick (12)**
**Meoncross School**


# Betrayal

The pain of betrayal enters my mind,
As if the Grim had himself signed,
The key to my body, mind and soul,
And handed it to the Devil as one whole.

The pain of betrayal from one of my friends,
Bleeds inside me, it may never end,
My friend left me as I screamed for help,
As they left all the pain in their souls to me they dealt.

In time of course it will all go away,
My hatred will no more, far stray,
Time will save me from this unruly fate,
A life of anguish, a life of hate.

**Gilbert Cross (13)**
**Meoncross School**

# Dreamworld

Far up high on the highest cloud,
Is Dreamworld standing great and proud.
As you enter the stairs you climb,
To the golden doors that sparkle and shine.
The first thing you see is a light pink sky,
And tiny purple birds swiftly they fly.
There are chocolate streams and cotton candy trees,
And millions of flowers with kind honeybees.
If you jump up tall and really try,
You may even take off and fly.
As you soar through the air you may even see,
A floating pig, a cat or three.
If you look up at the sky of pinks
A rainbow stretched on the sky then sinks,
Next to the shimmering pot of gold,
A rainbow pool, warm not cold.
As you begin to dive straight in
You feel dizzy, with shivers and trembling skin.
You were in Dreamworld, but now instead
You're in your soft and fluffy bed.

**Melissa Bailey (12)**
Meoncross School

# Haikus Menu

A potato shell
Vegetable soup with some bread
Prawn cocktail with toast

A lovely mixed grill
Sausages and chips and peas
Half a roast chicken

Goat's cheese and biscuits
Apple and barley pudding
Chocolate ice cream.

**Anthony Sims (12)**
Meoncross School

# Apples Galore

Give me apples,
Red, yellow, green,
Golden, spotted, juicy,
Or any in my dreams.

My mum has one for breakfast,
My dad has one for tea,
My dog has one that makes him fast
And I have one for me.

My friends give me their apples
And I give them my cheese,
The school gives out free samples,
Now we won't get a disease.

**Samantha Hoffman  (12)**
**Meoncross School**


# Chocolate

Chocolate is a perfect food,
Puts you in the best of moods,
But chocolate does smack my lips,
A minute in my mouth and a lifetime on my hips,
You will not get spots if you eat lots and lots,
It won't make you fat, whoever thought of that?
Five bars a day is all you need,
Instead of fruit eat chocolate feed,
Chocolate is a perfect food,
Puts you in the best of moods,
In fact it will make you thin,
So come on everybody let's join in!

**Jessica Budnyj  (12)**
**Meoncross School**

# McCann's Murder Mince

Serves - 1 school

*You will need:*
Oven
180 dishes
Puff pastry
Pot
Roast potatoes

*Ingredients:*
1 Dash of detective
I minuscule of murderer
180 vats of victim
2 whacks of witness
180 pints of poison (tasteless)
180 laxative tablets (tasteless)
180 kilos of mince
1 school

*Method:*
Place the shot of school in the oven and add a little detective, murderer, laxative tablets, a pint of poison in each dish, mix with mince then add a drop of radioactive sauce, 180 vats of victim and a couple of witnesses then cook for 30 minutes. Then put the roast potatoes and puff pastry in the oven and cook for 15 minutes. Then take out of oven and you're ready to eat McCann's murder mince.

**Ryan McCann  (12)**
**Meoncross School**


# The Owl

It was a dark night.
Something flickered past, so bright.
It wasn't a star, nor the moon,
But something that lurked among the gloom.
It swooped again and missed its prey,
It will be back again another day.

**Samantha Buck  (11)**
**Moyles Court School**

# Terror

The patter of feet,
On that New York street,
The birds are flying,
A girl is crying,
The smoke above,
The broken love,
Destruction is here,
Giving its evil leer,
The people stall,
The towers fall,
Only a few people who are now despised,
Made the evil mist arise,
The world has broken,
Terror has spoken,
Terrorists seem never finished,
The peace has gone completely diminished,
These sickening people must be stopped,
Before the world is sliced and chopped.

**Steven Lucas (13)**
**Moyles Court School**


# Animals

Animals are becoming more rare,
Yes, I really do care!
Those lovely, poor creatures are all being killed,
And all that pain they create but obviously they don't relate
That life is such a precious thing you only have one chance,
Those people must be stopped, these priorities are top,
They must not make anymore money,
Then they will not find it so funny!
If they were living the life they were killing,
Then they would do it no more.

**Sarah Dickinson (12)**
**Moyles Court School**

# Silence

The night was silent,
No voice was heard,
Not even a squeak,
From a mouse or bird.

The night was loud,
The music blared out,
The silence was broken,
So we all danced about.

The morning was silent,
Not a rustle from a tree,
Not even a buzz
From a buzzing bee.

The morning was loud,
The alarm clock kept ringing,
You could not hear yourself think,
For the church choir singing.

**Kirsty Osborne (13)**
**Moyles Court School**


# Where Was He?

The postman came, the letter box opened,
The frightful words, 'He is lost in the field.'
My heart sank deeply.
Where was he? Where was he?

Soldiers marching up and down,
People dying all around.
Cries came from wives and children.
Where was he? Where was he?

Helicopters flying here and there,
The sound of guns got closer and closer,
A pain in the head, a shot in the leg,
He's dead. He's dead.

**Emma Chapman-Burnett (12)**
**Moyles Court School**

# Emotions

My anger is coloured bloody red,
I feel all numb and I want to get it out.
It tastes like flaming hot chilli sauce,
Sounds like two trains colliding.
It smells like damp, musty mud.

When I am happy, I feel like
Skipping across long, crispy grass.
My happiness looks like
A large bunch of fresh roses.
It tastes like sweet candy sticks
And smells like fresh bread.
The colour of my happiness is
Like a bright sun.
It sounds like everybody is cheering for me.

**Sapphire Sax  (11)**
**Moyles Court School**

# War

S oldiers march up and down
E ven Hitler can frown
C aptured soldiers waiting to be set free
O ld men dying slowly
N ever get left behind
D ying can be painful, you will find

W ar is a dangerous devotion
O fficers can die in an explosion
R ed people are put in a sack
L oved ones can never come back
D ead people all around

W ater is pulling a crowd
A rmies preparing to come back in
R unning is a frightful thing.

**Olivia Annet-Short  (12)**
**Moyles Court School**

# II Gulf War

In Iraq the women are crying
Over their loved ones dying.

The soldiers are going to war
To kill those against the law.

Bullets go flying over their heads
While we sleep in our comfy beds.

The soldiers are trying to catch Saddam Hussein
To try and get rid of this horrible pain.

The army is back
To start the attack.

The fight for good has started
As the squadrons are parted.

Finally we have won
But the fighting still goes on.

The civilians are hurt
As their bodies hit the dirt.

**Dalton North  (12)**
**Moyles Court School**


# War Time

War time is terrible.
The fighting, the death breaks my heart.
Families destroyed, homes destroyed
And the terrorists do it for religion, for faith.

War time is terrible
And there is nowhere to hide.
The guns stop suddenly,
I feel really tense.
My heart's pounding hard,
When I saw, they were dead.

**Joseph Drew  (13)**
**Moyles Court School**

# Olympics 2004

The Olympics was full of classic moments
Some joyful and some heart-wrenching
We all saw Paula's dream die in seconds
And gallant Gebresalasie in his Olympic final.

The rowing was one of those wonderful moments
The coxless four awesome as ever
Pinsent and company winning on the line
From the ever-present Canadians who did so fine.

Who could forget Kelly Holmes
Against all odds taking gold
From the likes of Mutola and Ceplak
In two exhilarating races she won so bold.

In the mighty heat of Athens
All the athletes did all they could
On the track or in the pool
All those athletes who took part probably knew they would.

These were a few of the wonderful moments
Which in years to come will be known as classics
There might not be a better Olympics
Because this Olympics was truly wonderful.

**Ryan Saunders  (13)**
**Moyles Court School**


# Love

Love is a strange, wonderful thing.
Love lifts you up where you belong.
Love makes you feel special
Like someone loves you in the big wide world.
Life is nothing without love.
Love can make you angry and sad at the same time.
Love makes you do crazy things.
Love is so incredible.
Love is so great there are no words to describe how.

**Jenny Smith  (13)**
**Moyles Court School**

# Don't Drink And Drive

Driving through the midnight mist
Along the windy road, through the woods
I felt dizzy and ill.
My eyelids started to fall.

I saw a vision coming towards me.
It came closer and closer,
Until I realised what the vision was,
A man cycling up the road.

Then I blinked and he had gone.
I got out the car to see where he was,
Until I realised that he was not cycling anymore
I didn't know what I had done.

Suddenly I heard police sirens,
My whole body was out of control,
I didn't know what to do
So I drove away.

Now my vision was going fuzzy,
All I was focusing on was getting home,
But I was alone
In my car with no sense of direction.

But then I saw flashing lights
Coming right towards me,
I didn't know what to do.
I just kept driving, trying to get home.

I was now unconscious,
I had killed two people,
I had committed manslaughter,
I was drunk and I had been drinking.

**James Smith (13)**
**Moyles Court School**

# Sunrise

The alarm disturbed my peaceful sleep,
Now I would never know the ending to my perfect dream,
Sarah pulled the duvet off me,
It was cruel but it was the only thing that worked,
I forced myself out of bed,
I grabbed my wool jumper,
Sarah and I made our way up the cold, stone steps,
The house was quiet,
Everyone was asleep.
As we opened the door we made sure not to wake anyone.
We sat in the conservatory in silence,
We had the perfect view of the sea.
An hour passed as we waited,
Then the slightest ray of sun appeared,
We ran out of the house,
The morning air was cold,
We ran over the sand dunes
And down onto the beach.
No one was in sight,
The ocean was calm,
Mist gathered at each end of the beach,
It crept slowly towards us,
The only sound was the squawking of the seagulls,
The sun rose over the sea,
It was magical,
The sun looked like a ball of fire across the ocean,
The sand was cold between my toes,
I did not need to know the ending of my dream,
The dream was right here.

**Mali Griffiths  (13)**
**Moyles Court School**

# When Will It Stop?

Bombs flying,
Children dying,
Soldiers crying.

Iraq attacks,
The US strikes back,
Bullets land with an almighty crack.

Guns ablaze,
The heat is a haze,
I hope all this killing is just a phase.

Houses burn,
Children learn,
Stomachs churn.

The sky turns grey,
This will never pay,
I pray to the end of the day.

When will this stop?
When will the guns drop?
Too many people have been shot.

Gases spread,
Women dead,
We would be OK, the President said.

When will this stop?
When will it end?
But it won't.
A problem like this is too big to mend.

**Giles Watson  (13)**
**Moyles Court School**

# Hunter Trials

It was the day of the hunter trials,
I had to get up early.
Micki, my pony, had to look her best.
I brushed her and brushed her
Until she shone like the sun,
Then we loaded her into the trailer
And drove away into the distance.
It seemed like hours until we finally arrived.
Bumping down the track,
Poor old Micki must have nearly fallen over.
We brought her out into the big open field,
Her head picked up,
Her ears pricked,
As her nostrils flared.
Micki loved cross-country,
Flying over the jumps,
She looked like an elegant bird.
We did the whole course
And went round it clear.
Overall, we came eighth out of sixty,
Which for our first hunter trials
Was more than I could have asked.
Horses are truly wonderful creatures.
They are swift and elegant
And have such loving hearts,
But you have to gain their trust.
Micki, my pony, is so loving to me,
And I will love her back for as long as life shall be.

**Gemma Fraser  (13)**
**Moyles Court School**

# The Olympic Games

The time has come,
All the training has been done,
For the Olympic Games have come,
For one race, with a lot of training.

The gun is fired and you're off,
Power and stamina in your stride.
You feel as if you're unstoppable,
Until you are outrun by other athletes.

The bell goes,
You give it your all,
Whatever you do, you cannot lose your cool.
You pass another athlete, and another . . .

It is the home straight,
You can see the finish line.
Before you know it, you've won.
You know your job has been done.

**George Soan (13)**
**Moyles Court School**


# Tonight And Tomorrow

It's windy, it's bright,
It's going to be lovely tonight.
It will be bad in the morning
When everyone is snoring.
When they get up, they always
Have a cup of tea.
It's always nice to have
A bite of a biscuit too.
When you go out to get some more
You always lock the door.

**Robert Fraser (11)**
**Moyles Court School**

# A Precious Gift

A lot of different people
Will walk in and out of our lives,
Opening doors into friendship.
But only true friends
Will leave treasured memories
With their footprints in our hearts.

Love and honour them,
Look after them
Like a precious gift
And they always
Give you a lift,
Inside and outside.
In return I can share
My laughter and tears,
In my thoughts they will always be there.
There are no people,
Just friends.

**Grace Sheppard  (13)**
Moyles Court School


# Sea Spray

On a windy day
I go for a walk at the bay.
I see a ray,
Then feel a spray
Of a raging sea
Where
The waves are crashing,
Smashing
Against the rocky shore
As the rain begins to pour,
More and more.

**Alexander Haigh  (11)**
Moyles Court School

# Animals

Animals are everywhere, up in the sky and under the stairs,
Some are big and some are small, but who really cares,
Because we love them all.

Spiders are scary, horses are cute,
And then there are owls with a very loud hoot.
Some animals are rough, some animals are smooth,
But whatever they're like, they still grow and move.

Some animals are wild, some are kept as pets,
Some like to keep dry, and some just love to get wet.
Some like the warmth, and some like the cold,
But they are all living, just like mould.

Some live in houses, some live in forests,
Some live in rivers, and some live in florists!

**Anna Peachey (11)**
**Moyles Court School**


# Harvest Festival

The barns are full,
The tractors pull
The trailers stacked with bales of hay.
The people work in the fields all day.

In the church, the pumpkins arrive
After battling through the summer months to survive.
The fruit is big, the fruit is round,
The carrots are orange and they've been found
Growing in the ground.

The melons are big, the melons are green,
And that's my harvest festival scene.

**Henry Bowen (10)**
**Moyles Court School**

# Global Warming

Global warming is a terrible thing,
People chopping down trees just to get energy,
And by doing this, destroying the environment.
The birds, animals and humans all suffer.

The cold and hot will be going extreme,
Because we send out harmful gases.
Why don't we use the streams
For power, transport and bathing?

The water from sea, rivers and oceans,
Could be used to power cities,
And it would mean no harmful gases.
We could use a number of other things.

Like wind, thermoelectric and solar power.
But there is another way of stopping global warming,
And this way is to walk, jog, or bike,
Rather than use the car.

**Matthew Haynes  (13)**
**Moyles Court School**


# Cats

Cats are cute and cats are sweet,
They climb up trees and chase bluebells.
They sleep in shoes and crawl in holes,
Their teeth are sharp and white as well.
They jump on tables and walk on walls,
They're clean and graceful in so many ways.
I don't know much, but all I know is
I love them and they love me,
But once their minds are made up,
They ignore any plea.

**Michelle Long  (13)**
**Moyles Court School**

# All About Me

My name is Jake
And I am so cool,
I do love cake
And I sometimes play the fool.

I do have friends,
I'm not a loner,
My name is Jake
And I'm a bit of a joker.

I do like football,
I don't like spiders,
I do like chocolate
And I like Fruit Winders.

I like to watch Arsenal play,
I don't like Chelsea any day.
Now you've heard a bit about me,
Drop in sometime for a cup of tea.

**Jake Harris (12)**
**Moyles Court School**


# Football

Football, football, lovely football,
Kicked, flicked
Into a net.
*Goal, goal, goal.*
The ball rolls
On the ground,
Throw it, kick it,
Take it away and the whistle will go.
And that's the end of the game.

**Thomas Welch (12)**
**Moyles Court School**

# Emotions

*Anger*
My anger is black, like a black hole,
It tastes vile, such as a lot of spinach.
I think it's like blood in the mouth,
Sounds like a cat fighting for its life.
It's sharp and scratches my mouth,
Looks like a giant man-eating shark.

*Jealousy*
My jealousy is green and brown like a swamp,
It tastes like ashes left from the fire,
Smells like sulphurous rock from the volcano,
Looks like the apocalypse.
Sounds like a tornado blowing down over everything,
Looks like a person that just died.

**Matthew Head  (11)**
**Moyles Court School**


# Poachers

Tigers are losing their numbers,
Their population is starting to plummet,
Only 5,000 of them are left.
These big, lovely cats
Are dying night and day
Due to horrible poachers.
Tigers are such graceful creatures.
There are loads of things they could teach us,
But they can't, because of poachers
Ending their lives too early.
Just for a little money,
They destroy the tigers' souls.

**Shaunie Huzzey  (12)**
**Moyles Court School**

# War . . .

Shells are exploding,
The rain is pattering,
Those screaming voices
Fill my nightmares.

Sea-green gas leaking into the air,
Men dropping like flies before me,
Coughing, spluttering, staggering blindly,
Praying they won't be found by the enemy.

Petrified men
Retreat away from the bombs.
The fearsome enemy strikes out,
Showing no mercy.

Men marched asleep,
In disbelief,
Hoping, praying
That they'll last another day.

**Katie Roath  (13)**
**Regents Park Girls' School**

# How?

*(For my beloved grandfather, Jaswant Singh Grewal)*

The ones you love with heart and soul
are the ones that should never leave you,
but when death takes them,
what should you do?
When all happiness is gone,
and you're drowning in sadness,
what should you do?
How do you carry on?
How?

**Balvinder Sidhu  (13)**
**Regents Park Girls' School**

# The Waiting

The tension is building,
While we are waiting to charge.
We're standing in a lengthy line,
With people in front and behind,
As far as the eye can see.

Then suddenly, the officer shouts,
'Charge, men, charge!'
We all run towards the enemy.

Then I heard a 'bang',
I look down, I've been shot,
There is blood
Pouring from my left leg.

I can't stand any longer,
I collapse with pain.
I close my eyes.
I never opened them again.

**Charlotte Eckett  (13)**
**Regents Park Girls' School**


# War Poem

My body armour is on and I'm ready to fight.
Hearing gunshots and seeing men dying,
I taste my fear.

Dying and killing,
Blood is spilling.

I'm lying dead,
And yet,
I don't feel like a hero,
So don't forget . . .

**Kirsten Tarrant  (13)**
**Regents Park Girls' School**

# War

Silence all around until the enemy attacks,
Only the immense shrieking of guns and dying,
Men can be heard for miles.
When this war is over,
Will this be a peaceful world?

All they see is mounds of shells, on a sea of bodies,
Soldiers mourn when their friends don't return.
Will this world ever be the same again
After this awful war?

Years go by, still missing their families,
Just waiting day after day, to be sent over the top.
Will this war ever end?
That's all I want to know.

**Megan Robinson (13)**
**Regents Park Girls' School**


# The War Poem

War is terrifying,
You worry about the battle,
From dawn through to night.

You hear the sound of guns.
Has the war begun?

Everyone grabs their weapons,
And starts falling into line.
The paranoid soldiers running,
Running out of time.

Then over the top,
Shooting to save their lives,
Running towards the enemy,
Wondering if they'll survive.

**Katie Muddiman (13)**
**Regents Park Girls' School**

# If My Mum Were A Cherry

If my mum were a cherry,
Her taste would be delicious, mouth-watering and sweet,
So when you go down to the market,
Why not buy yourself a treat?
She will be waiting to be picked,
Because that lucky person
Is going to do the right thing.

Her red velvet skin
Will shine in the sun,
All the other cherries are jealous,
Because this cherry is Number One,
So that means it's got to be my mum.

**Emily Street (12)**
**Regents Park Girls' School**

# My Sister

If my sister were a panther,
She would be shadowy and beautiful like the night sky.
Mysterious and dark,
Long and quiet, but sharp like a knife,
But very angry and argumentative, like a President.

**Harriet Wiley (13)**
**Regents Park Girls' School**

# If My Mum!

If my mum was an animal,
She'd be a tall, but thin, bear!
With long paws and brown fur
That would shine in the light,
But shimmer in the dark.

**Penny Topley-Watts (12)**
**Regents Park Girls' School**

# My Sister

Hair like vermicelli,
With a real flat belly.
Loves to eat jelly,
Certainly not smelly.
Sits in front of the telly
Would never wear a welly.

Goes out to play
Each and every day,
Will never stray,
With Mum she likes to stay.
Her mood is never grey,
She's happy all the way.

When the work is done,
She likes to run,
Has great fun
Stuffing an iced bun.
Will never weigh a ton,
She's a skinny little one.

Who could she be?
My sister, Sophie!

**Grace Mwakisunga (11)**
**Regents Park Girls' School**


# My Sister

If my sister were an animal,
She would be a dolphin,
Bright blue and grey,
Smooth and soft,
Like aluminium, shiny and elegant.
She's exactly like my best friend.
She's out of date,
Like a 90-year-old granny.

**Louise Spicer (11)**
**Regents Park Girls' School**

# The Madness Of War

*Bang!*

My best friend drops to the ground.
He has been shot.
I now feel terrified of what may happen to me.
I don't want to fight,
I just want to run away and hide forever.
I don't want to be killing people,
Normal people like me and you,
But I have to fight,
I have to kill to defend my country.

**Jordan Klinko  (14)**
**Regents Park Girls' School**


# War

The war has just begun.
Men are fighting,
Many dying each day.
Men are scared of getting shot,
Hoping it's not their turn to go over the top.
Family at home missing them badly,
Hoping every day,
Carrying on sadly,
Wishing the war would end.

**Ella Scriven  (13)**
**Regents Park Girls' School**


# School Feelings

When someone says, 'No' I get upset.
When something is boring, I forget.
When I'm at school I learn,
Though with a distraction I turn.
That's how every child feels at school.

**Zoë O'Shea  (11)**
**Regents Park Girls' School**

# War Poem

I'm wondering what's happened to him.
Wondering if he's safe and alive.
I put on the news,
*Bang,* an explosion. I ask myself,
      Was he there?

I hope that my dear uncle is safe.
When I was born, he was out in Iraq,
Now I realise what stress
My family were going through.
      Is he coming back?

Every time there is news
That British soldiers have been held hostage, or killed,
I jump and become afraid
That such a brave man has lost his life.
      Is he dead?

He's back now, he survived.
I'm so glad he's home.
I run up and hug him
And give him a kiss.
      I'm so glad he's back.

**Chloe Crispin (13)**
**Regents Park Girls' School**


# My Mum

If my mum was a flower,
I think she would be a pansy,
Bright pinks and yellows
From summer through to winter,
Up early in the morning,
Ready for the day ahead.

**Stephanie Ward-Hannan (11)**
**Regents Park Girls' School**

# My Messy Room

If my sister's room was like mine,
It would have coloured paint stripes,
Reflecting light from the
Sunflower lamp at night.
Some sandy seashells,
A mouldy chipped cup,
Which my poor mother
Had tried to pick up.
A doll's head, a hair band,
And to my surprise,
A bold strip of tinsel
And a jar of glass eyes.
A rusty zip, broken,
A spider's leg, bent,
A chewed-up old pencil,
And a box with a dent.
It's a while since I've been there,
And I'm in no hurry to clean my room.

**Kiren Sandhu  (11)**
**Regents Park Girls' School**


# War Poem

As the guns fired again,
Jumping and screaming
We landed in a trench,
Crawling and cold.

People shout for help, in agony,
As bayonets slide through flesh.
For kingdom and country.

Our nightmare continues . . .

**Danielle Tribbeck  (13)**
**Regents Park Girls' School**

# My Life In War

My life flashes before my eyes,
The bullet,
Spinning towards me,
The pain hits me
Before the bullet itself.
My family,
My friends,
My sweetheart,
My last thoughts.
Survival is what I need,
Survival,
But the only option for me
In no-man's-land is -
Death.
God, take me now,
Keep my loved ones safe.
Let me fly,
Let me be the sacrifice
For my king and country.
Let me die for a reason.
Let me die in bravery.

**Kellie Hatcher  (13)**
**Regents Park Girls' School**


# My Sister

If my sister were a dancer,
She would be a ballerina,
As elegant as a swan.
She would dance around the house all day
With that grinning smile of hers.
She would get into loads of trouble,
And get out of it
With her cute puppy-dog eyes.

**Abigail Wall  (12)**
**Regents Park Girls' School**

# My Dad

If my dad were a toy, he'd be a robot,
Not colourful,
Made of silver metal,
Always working, never wasting time.
Working harder than a computer.

**Wendy Wong  (13)**
**Regents Park Girls' School**

# Tree

There he stands, bare,
As the last of his few leaves start to fall,
All of his elegant, copper-orange leaves leaving him, but why?
'It is autumn,' cries the great oak,
'You may have lost your copper-orange leaves,
But he who waits gains vibrant greens.'
'What is he on about?' the small silver birch asked the cherry tree.
'You will find out,' mumbled the cherry tree,
As her branches creaked in the breeze.

**Jemma Gilbert  (12)**
**Regents Park Girls' School**

# Bonfire

The fire crackles, the flames burn,
The children laugh, the heads all turn.

The fireworks lighting up the sky,
So many colours flashing by,
Red, yellow, pink and green,
There are so many to be seen.

**Rachel Harrison  (12)**
**Regents Park Girls' School**

## My Mum

My mum is very special to me,
She is always there for me,
She never lets me down.
When I am feeling ill,
She always makes me feel better.
If I need help, she is always there.
My mum has helped me through my childhood,
And always helps me through problems in my life.
I love my mum,
And I am glad I have the mum I have.

**Kirsty McGregor-Ritchie (12)**
Regents Park Girls' School


## Winter

The rain came down on a windswept day,
People rushed by with nothing to say.

The car lights flickered in the inky gloom,
Witches flew by, sat on their brooms.

Dark, heavy clouds became thicker and thicker,
The rain and wind started to bicker.

By the minutes and seconds my hands got number,
I don't know about you, but bring on the summer!

**Ella Dixon (13)**
Regents Park Girls' School


## My Rabbit

If my rabbit were a dog, she'd be a cocker spaniel,
Grey and grizzly,
Fuzzy like a teddy,
Small and sweet and rather naughty,
But really fast, so you could not catch her.

**Makada Mills (12)**
Regents Park Girls' School

# War!

*(Inspired by 'Dulce et Decorum est' by Wilfred Owen)*

The death, pain and destruction
I still can see
It comes from the earth beneath
From the blood that flowed
From the men who died and were never found!

'The war to end all wars'
It wasn't clear
From one war came another and another
It's never over
The loss of life is too great to keep doing this.

Every shot I take a life has been destroyed
A father, a husband, a son
These brave men die for the land or pride of another
Death to all that come
The guns firing
The shells dropping

Blood shod and lame the men march
Trying to remember why they fight, why they came
Just wishing, hoping they won't be the next
The next to be shot down dead, as there their comrade has been
Wanting to see their families, they struggle for life
For a dream
Now so far away they can barely see it

All they see as they close their eyes are bodies
Slung over the back of a wagon
Mouths gargling
Eyes red with blood
Then they question the old lie

To die for your country is an honour?

**Charlotte Gibbs  (13)**
**Regents Park Girls' School**

# War Poem

Innocent eyes watching the world fall to pieces,
People being attacked by others for no reason,
Why is it that war is the only answer?
Surely, there's another way?

Soldiers marching to their deaths,
Murdering the innocent before being murdered themselves,
They kill in many ways, bombs, guns and gas,
Conflict between rivals started this,
Is this the only way to end?

People waiting with baited breath,
Waiting to be told that their loved ones are dead,
They don't know what will happen next,
Children are crying, knowing that something is wrong,
This isn't the way their lives should be living.

The guiltless people stare at the sky,
Seeing planes fly over, carrying bombs
That will take them to their death,
Back at the battlefield the wounded are screaming for help,
But no one hears their pleas for help.

**Emma Burnett  (13)**
**Regents Park Girls' School**


# Wintertime

Wintertime is always cold,
Autumn plants look dirty and old,
The wind is strong as you can see,
I'll wrap up warm, nic-e-ly.

The dog is barking to come inside,
He's looking for a place to hide.
It's Christmas soon, I can't wait,
To reveal my presents, beyond all fate.

**Ellis Nichols  (13)**
**Regents Park Girls' School**

# War!

The clashing of thunder,
Like the dropping bombs
That litter the black skies,
Lit up only by the lightning and
Gunfire of a nearby battle.

Soldiers sent over the top
Come crashing down
Like the waves of
An angry storm.

The rain pouring down from above
Like flights of streaking bullets,
Clouds of gas swallowing up the troops
Of doomed men,
Soon to meet their death.

**Ruby Hart  (13)**
**Regents Park Girls' School**


# War Poem

Wet, oozing mud is sliding through
My cheap army boots.

I lie here waiting for the next shell to drop, the next man to die,
They replace us as though we are on tap.

Our generals say they back us,
But they live in stately homes, 35 miles away,
They do not care about how we live,
They view war as a game, if they are winning.

Thousands of men lose their lives by
Charging over the front line just to gain six inches of land.

I lost my comrade today, we could relate to each other,
Now I am here alone, like I came,
But I have a feeling I won't be going back.

**Hannah Willis  (13)**
**Regents Park Girls' School**

# Alone And Waiting

We stand still,
We stand all alone . . . waiting.
Watching skyscrapers of dreams
Crumble behind us,
As we wait alone.

We wait to be forgiven
For the evil doings we have perpetrated,
But Heaven turns to dust at the touch of fate that brought us here,
Leaving Hell open
To the sins we commit.
So we stand soulless,
Waiting or him to free us.

But we are bound in chains
To our worst nightmare:
A life of pain and sorrow,
Of killing and deceit
That we brought upon ourselves
When we let those tainted lies surge out of our mouths.

We killed and watched others suffer,
But when we came to lose one of our own,
We asked for pity,
But gained none.
So we blamed others for our actions.
We say they pressurised us,
But we fail to remember we have free will
And we did not have to play the puppet.

**Elizabeth Woodiwiss (13)**
**Regents Park Girls' School**

# The Eternal Pain

One year on,
The pain hasn't gone,
I close my eyes,
I see the devastation,
The faces of the dead,
Bloodshed.

Torn between life and death,
I was a murderer.
I saw the murdered,
I lost my family, friends,
I saw them suffer.

I still wish it was me
On the back of that wagon,
Piled as high as the trenches themselves,
Someone's son, someone's only love.

Now every night I close my eyes,
I see my brother die,
Slowly and quietly,
Gassed, killed, brutally,
I saw his face pleading
For me to save him.

Why won't the pain go?
When will I be freed from the painful memories?
When will my eternal pain stop?
Somehow, I know it will stay with me until the day I too die.

**Charlotte Fripp  (13)**
**Regents Park Girls' School**

# War Child

They said they'd bring us freedom.
A life. A future. A hope.
But all that they have brought us is a war
With which no one can cope.

Before, I had some sort of life.
We had happiness, despite our fear,
But then they came and stole it all,
And if we cry out for help, there is no one who will hear.

I will never forget the day they came.
They drove their tanks through our streets,
We fought with no one - we were too afraid,
But fear is nothing compared to the enormous price we paid.

No one in this country has limped free without loss.
Everyone is grieving for the tragic human cost
That we were forced to pay.

**Joanna Wroe  (14)**
**Regents Park Girls' School**


# War

The gunfire cackled through the night,
The flares lit up the sky,
The soldiers dying one by one,
Never to be seen again.

The deadly gas that crept silently,
The gas masks that protected,
But there's always one not fitted in time,
And yet another death.

But when the war is over finally,
Not everything is peaceful.
The families of soldiers lost
Can never be complete or happy.

**Emily Smith  (13)**
**Regents Park Girls' School**

# War Poem

Now: in modern wars,
One death is a tragedy -
Even the very thought.

But then: thousands had to die
To have an impact -
On even a sympathetic mind.

Now: war is postponed;
Peace treaties, alliances,
Are made to deflect
The very thought
Of murder, death and pain.

But then: war was inevitable;
Fought for just more glory - pride,
Greedy rulers, greedy for yet more splendour
On their own little cloud,
Much higher than any of ours.

**Céline Galloway (13)**
**Regents Park Girls' School**


# The Forest

The forest is my secret place,
The wind is delicate and calm,
Suddenly picking up a fast pace,
Brushing against my tender cheek.

The trees are beautiful and big,
Leaves as glamorous as a rose,
Never had a broken twig,
The trees are like my home, just as much as the squirrels.

The creatures in the forest are such a pain,
Not seen one as big as a lion,
The ants are just like an army of soldiers, all walking in one lane,
The forest is my secret place.

**Nishat Ahmed (12)**
**Regents Park Girls' School**

# Old Love

*(A conversation between Lady Carmel, a dancer, and the old man, a drinker)*

'Old woman dancing on stage,
Your graceful moves,
Young-hearted, unlike your age.
How I dig your grooves.'

'Old man, you flatter me,
But I cannot explain.
Those words which you shower me with,
I cannot complain.'

'Woman, come drink with me,
Make conversation,
Don't waste your energy,
Feel relaxation.'

'I must dance the night away
Or my manager will fill with rage,
For if I want to here stay,
I must dance upon my stage.'

'Oh, I don't want to bribe,
Your wrinkled face, but twinkling eyes,
I can't say the love inside
Which I feel for you, to my surprise.'

'You may shower me with compliments,
And sweet-smelling flowers,
But not with all the chocolates,
May I leave, I haven't the powers.'

'Please, for I am old and lonely,
My house is as cold as stone.
You, my precious, can make it more homely,
So I am not left alone.'

'No matter how I long for that,
I must bid farewell,
For I must prepare for my departure,
Therefore leave, and remember, I am Lady Carmel.'

**Ruth Murray & Iesha Churcher (12)**
**Regents Park Girls' School**

# My Garden

Some would say it's a jungle of wild creatures,
Others would think of it with lovely features.
Some would like it, some would hate it,
But it's my family's and what we create.

The flowers blossoming attract the eye,
Until large, heavy footballs come rushing by.
The sense of happiness, peace and joy,
Is crashed in one day by a little boy.

A little girl helps with the attack,
A cycling nightmare with a crash, bang, smack!
In this zoo, this extravagant thing,
Comes much joy, the joy it may bring.

This enclosure has ups and downs,
But to explore it is quite profound.
With fun, laughter and much, much riot,
Is a lonely place, where all is quiet.

Some would say it's a jungle of wild creatures,
Others would think of it with splendid features.
Some would love it, some would hate,
But it's my family's and what we create.
It's the best, most wondrous place,
Me and my garden, face to face.

**Katrina Loizou (12)**
**Regents Park Girls' School**


# My Mum

If my mum was an animal, she'd be a cat.
Mixed brown and ginger hair,
Smooth as a coat of feathers,
Smart and clean, just like a queen,
But always out exploring.

**Gabi Suliemani (13)**
**Regents Park Girls' School**

# Bang . . . Bang . . . Bang!

Christmas is tomorrow, 25th December,
But I am still stuck here
Amongst people, men I don't even know.
*Bang . . . bang . . . bang!* There it goes again.
I want to go home.
It's all wet and windy,
It's all cold and suffocating,
There is nothing to eat.
Why . . . why . . . oh why am I here alone?
All my friends were blown up,
The Germans killed my friends.
Where is my wife?
I need my wife.
*Bang . . . bang . . . bang . . .*
We scream, shout and shiver,
For we wonder what is going to happen next.
Please, help . . . help . . . help.

**Sukdev Bhakar  (14)**
**Regents Park Girls' School**


# My Friends

My friends are an important part of me,
They make me feel special; they make me feel free.
They help me out when things are tough,
They make me feel better when I'm feeling rough.
They lend me things; they play fun games,
They're not horrible, they don't call me names.
They stand up for me, they don't desert me,
They fight back when people hurt me.
They know the whole me inside out,
I know they will always be there, without a doubt.
My friends are wicked, my friends are great,
I hope everyone has friends like my mates.

**Eloise Lavington  (13)**
**Regents Park Girls' School**

# There's Nothing Left But Sadness!

Bullets fly swiftly through the air,
My mind thinks of nothing but home.
I cringe as the sound of guns bursts my ears,
The birds once here have now gone!
There's nothing left but sadness!

I take position as the cold air stings my eyes,
I hear men shouting, *'Gas! Gas!'*
The panic begins. The sound of terror
Fills my mind with coldness and evil.
There's nothing left but sadness!

The machine guns cry out their tears,
As the snowflakes fill the air.
All of a sudden, there's silence,
Christmas has come upon us.
There's nothing left but sadness!

As we join and unite as one,
We kick the ball. With joy we rage,
We finally have come together
For that day which I won't forget!

**Sheralee Walsh (13)**
**Regents Park Girls' School**

# Seasons

Winter is cold,
Frosted and frozen.
Autumn is gloomy,
Leaves falling by the dozen.
Summer is bright,
Warm and heated.
Spring is a time of hope,
Then everything is repeated.

**Heather Bilsby (13)**
**Regents Park Girls' School**

# On The Subject Of War

Christmas is coming in a few weeks' time,
But I am standing by the filthy and unbearable stagnant trench,
Wondering why we are fighting with such
Hate and fear for some worthless land?
Land that is far away from our loved ones . . .
Even though we know this war is pointless . . .
It's time to go to the killing fields located in no-man's-land
And fight for England to retain our honour and pride.
Out of the gloom
The silence strikes us,
One by one!

**Amina Shadab  (13)**
**Regents Park Girls' School**


# My Rabbit

If my rabbit were a deep, dark forest,
I would spend my life there.
He is as bright as the bright stars at night.
He is as pretty as a rose that has just bloomed.
He looks as young as when we first chose him.

**Sophie Burke  (12)**
**Regents Park Girls' School**


# The Dolphin

In the sun,
Jewels gleam on her body.
Playing with the fish,
Leaping with the seals,
Swimming with the stars
All night long.
Sleep with other dolphins
Until the fire star comes out to play.

**Kara Cuthbertson  (12)**
**Regents Park Girls' School**

## Scared Stiff

I'm terrified about going over the top,
For I know I could die with one shot.
The men around me are dirty and cold,
But carry on being brave and bold.
We are here, squatting in the dirt,
Many with injuries, tired or hurt.
Many wanting to go home
To their loving, warm family.
Bombs dropping all around,
Men are ducking underground.
*Bang!*
I wonder if I'm going to see my family again.

**Catherine Ballard  (13)**
**Regents Park Girls' School**


## Great Minds

Great minds think alike,
Like a pair of shoes.
They go everywhere together
And know just what to do.
That's why great minds think alike,
Like me and you.

**Danielle Roles  (12)**
**Regents Park Girls' School**


## My Cat

If my cat were a person, she would be a punk,
As painful as pins,
Minging like a mouldy sock,
Scary like Guy Fawkes,
But loving inside.

**Erin Mattingly  (11)**
**Regents Park Girls' School**

# Love

Love can give you feelings,
Feelings that you've never ever owned in your life . . .

Love can hurt you deep inside,
Maybe feels like a lifetime scar that will never ever go away . . .

Love is the deepest, most darkest secret that nobody,
Yet everybody needs to know about . . .

Love is like a sacred possession,
It takes over your life in a matter of seconds . . .

Love fills you with a kind of warmth,
That isn't the same as a hot water bottle . . .

Love has nothing to moan about,
Although if you think about it, your whole life finally draws
                                                    to the same thing . . .

There is nothing more about love that I can say,
Except that it's never, ever perfect . . .

And when you fall in love,
There is nothing you can ever do about it . . .

Never ever . . .

**Laura Ashton  (12)**
**Regents Park Girls' School**


# The Star Of A Sister

If my sister were a star,
She would twinkle all night
Till morning's first light.
Shine so bright,
Throughout the night.

**Mariyam Khan  (12)**
**Regents Park Girls' School**

# Forced

Forced to be blind,
The dying soldiers, coughing up their insides
Is too much to bear,
As they collapse to the ground, dead.
Not a soul respects them,
Tossed onto a heap,
Never to be remembered again.
Why should this happen?

Forced to be deaf,
Gas shells battering your ear,
Like a huge, poisonous drumstick,
Panic. You can't find your mask,
Armies of green cloud defeat you,
Blanketed by a silent enemy.
Is this right?

Forced to believe lies,
This is not glorious or patriotic,
Is mass murder beautiful?
Honour, duty, if you believe that,
Then you'll believe anything.
War. Think again.

**Hannah Doswell (14)**
**Regents Park Girls' School**


# Fun In The Sun

Happy days on the beach
With my best friend, Grace.
We are like dolphins swimming in the sea,
Turning, diving and jumping,
For everyone to see.
These memories I'll remember forever.

**Tara Wing (12)**
**Regents Park Girls' School**

# Waiting

Armed and ready,
We wait.
The days bleed together,
Shaking and shivering,
Rain soaks us,
Fatigue drowns us,
Destroying our strength.

No idea of how long
We stand waiting,
Absolutely frozen,
Not knowing what is real,
Or a figment of a
Delusional mind.

Time flows through our fingers,
As one we stand,
Armed and ready,
Waiting.

**Tiffany Heasman (14)**
**Regents Park Girls' School**


# My Dad

If my dad was a car, he would be a Ferrari,
Bright red, or fluorescent yellow,
Shiny and smooth.
Small and fast and rather dangerous,
Hip, cool and very fashionable.

**Yolanda Buxey (12)**
**Regents Park Girls' School**

# Flashbacks

Stumbling through the thick, never-ending gas,
I grasp for someone, anyone to help me.
Fumbling for my gas mask, my air is running short,
Death and drowning men surround me.

Blind, deaf and wounded,
I limp on back to the trenches,
Knowing that death will have to wait,
Ready to take me another time.

A cloud of flame shoots up behind me,
The earth leaps, the blast thundering in my ears.
The horrific scene paralyses me,
But I awaken myself to my senses, and take cover.

As I sit here, warm and toasty by the fire,
These flashes of war still haunt me,
As if I was there only yesterday,
Waiting for my death, praying for no more.

**Summer Medway  (13)**
**Regents Park Girls' School**


# My Goldfish

If my goldfish were a dress, it would be a flamenco dress.
Bright colours, bold and beautiful,
Smooth like silk,
Long, graceful and very pretty,
Shining brightly when they move.

**Ella Green  (12)**
**Regents Park Girls' School**

# Haunting Dreams

Flowers, gravestones and old gas masks,
The forgotten graveyard,
The explosions still haunt my dreams,
Dead bodies, flying feet in the air,
Bad memories.

Poppies, inscriptions and war helmets,
Ancient shell-holes,
I remember the gas attack,
Explosions illuminate the sky like lightning,
Bad memories.

Grass, coffins and bursts of freedom,
No more bombs,
I remember the exhilaration,
Sighs of relief, I'm alive,
Good memories.

**Jemma Gammon (13)**
**Regents Park Girls' School**


# My Mum

My mum is like a smiling, cuddly teddy,
Soft and warm,
Smiling like the sun,
Elegant and kind.
She is always loving and caring,
Just like a teddy bear.

**Sophie Harris (11)**
**Regents Park Girls' School**

# This Lonely Trench

I feel so cold and cramped
In this lonely trench.
My bed is dirty and so damp
In this lonely trench.

I have no food or any water
In this lonely trench.
There is no warmth or heat
In this lonely trench.

I have no friends or family
In this lonely trench.
I feel so afraid and so scared
In this lonely trench.

I may be dead or I may be not
But I will always be
In this lonely trench.

**Rachel Richings  (13)**
**Regents Park Girls' School**


# If My Mum Were A Fruit

If my mum were a fruit,
She would be a raspberry,
Tasting sweet and juicy.
She would feel as soft
As a fluffy white cloud.
She would be red,
Like a rich velvet coat.

**Danielle Winnicott  (11)**
**Regents Park Girls' School**

# Gone

I walk through the calm, dry field
And can't believe what happened here before.
I stare and stare, stare and stare,
With utter wonderment and awe.

A zone of mist clouds my memory,
As I see the bombs hiss softly.
'Cover! Cover! Gas! Gas!'
I throw myself behind a man
To save myself from a terrible death.

I prod the man to wake him,
But all he does is move a few inches.
I realise that this man saved my life
And I try to carry him over my shoulders,
But as I try, all I do is stumble.
And I now understand that this is the fate of a soldier.
Lost, dead and gone.

**Melissa Rungien  (13)**
**Regents Park Girls' School**


# Ode To War

The pitch-black sky,
Lit up by explosions.
The thick green gas
Lolling around me obscenely.

The rotting corpses
Lying beside me.
They are the lucky ones
To be free of all the pain.

My blood-filled hatred
Rising with every gunshot.
The anguish, the desperation, suffocates me.
Oh why do these memories torment me so?

**Rong Zhang  (13)**
**Regents Park Girls' School**

# Feelings Of War

War is a cruel and terrifying time,
Shooting and wounding with explosive mines.
War-torn bodies in the soldier's path,
Many going months without a bath.

Grimy trenches filled with vermin and dirt,
All getting shot, injured and hurt.
Rattling bullets scatter past my eyes,
Running away, I hear people's cries.

Who will help me? I'm all alone,
Wishing and wanting to go home.
Every man fighting for himself,
None of us in good health.

Loved ones years on, bereft of their sons,
Have cherished photos of their loved ones.
Robbed of their brave soldiers.
War is cruel! No mercy!

**Lauren Scriven  (13)**
**Regents Park Girls' School**


# The Soul

The soul is a thing inside that holds your emotion.
The soul is a thing that makes you feel
For things that you see or hear.
The best thing is that I can laugh and cry
And be happy and sad, because I have a soul in me.
The soul is said to live forever, therefore
Is eternal and lives after you die.
Inside the heart is where the soul lives.
The soul is a special thing
That is not to be sold or traded,
This is a sin.

**Sian Neave  (12)**
**Regents Park Girls' School**

# Harrison

A gentle soul, not capable of a word,
But his eyes pull you in.
Hands not as big as a bottle cap,
Clutching one finger,
But his eyes pull you in.
His mind is still a blank canvas,
But his eyes pull you in.
He's passed to me and
I cradle him in my arms,
I am now dependent on him
And his soft, podgy cheeks.
I tickle him and he opens just one eye,
But his eyes pull you in.
All he needs in one room,
A little baby.
Tiny baby Harrison.

**Amber Badger-Bell (12)**
**Regents Park Girls' School**


# War

I am suffocating and cannot breathe,
Another bombardment coming.
'Help!' I shout, as I begin to heave,
No gas mask, I hear drumming.

My eyes are blinded by the brightness.
What is happening?
I feel wheezy, there is nothing I can do,
Still no mask, I still hear ringing . . .

I awake, startled. Where am I?
Back in the hospital, with another nightmare.
Another flashback of that night, I dare not sigh,
The doctors will ask, and I shall not share.

**May Tsang (13)**
**Regents Park Girls' School**

# Another One To Add To The Tally

Fire-red and burnt orange
As the sun slips into slumber.
The conflict still does not cease.
No-man's-land - a sea of dead bodies,
A military graveyard.
As gunfire claims more,
They perish before us
Like wilting flowers,
Before hitting the mud-laden earth.
Another one to the tally.
Another wife widowed,
Waiting for that knock at the door.
Bombs fly high, but bombs fall hard.
As blasts of reds and oranges
Catapult human cannonballs
Shooting through the war sky,
Like a shooting star.
But this shooting star screams in pain
As he is charred to ash.
Another one to add to the tally.
Another fatherless child,
Because Daddy is not coming home.

How many more will be added to the tally?

**Emma Tweney  (13)**
**Regents Park Girls' School**

# My Sister

If my sister was a flower, she would be a lily,
She would be blooming all day long.
She would have the perfect little smile.
She would grow so big and beautiful,
As if she couldn't stop blooming.
She would be the most perfect little flower in the world.

**Manpreet Roopra  (12)**
**Regents Park Girls' School**

# Gas!

Gas, gas, gas,
Running and rumbling,
Sounds of a dying cause,
Footsteps and fumbling,
Ding in this painful war.

Gas, gas, gas.
'Masks on lads.'
We pull out as best we can,
Smiling and trying
To make it not so bad.

Gas, gas, gas,
Thunder in the north,
Thunder in the south,
Thunder in the east,
Thunder in the west,
Everything seems so dead.

Gas, gas, gas,
What's the point?
Why are we here?
Trudging on with painful joints,
Trudging, probably to our deaths.
Sickly war, death and disaster,
And we all call again,
'Gas, gas, gas.'

**Jessica Radford  (13)**
**Regents Park Girls' School**


# My Mum

If my mum were a jumper, she'd be amazing,
With bright blue eyes,
Her skin is so smooth,
Like a baby's bottom,
And she is beautiful.
That's my mum.

**Vicki Norman  (12)**
**Regents Park Girls' School**

# Gas Attack

'Take cover! Cover!' someone yells.
We stumble across in the dark.
The dark goes mad, it heaves!
It raves!
It rushes at us in giant strides,
Men glued behind mounds,
There is no escape!

Like a surging sea
It swallows us,
It pounds, it crushes, and it tears to pieces,
We must stay here!
There is no escape!

Like lightning the thought comes to me,
I shoot as flat as a fish,
Clawing for cover,
I open my eyes and see a man,
A wounded man?
A dead man?

I push under the coffin,
Death himself lies in it.
Coffins and corpses lie strewn about,
They have been killed once before
Hiding us! Saving us!

'Gas, gas, gas, pass it on.'
My mask will decide between life and death.
I stumble as I put it on,
Like a big jellyfish
It floats into our shell hole,
Surrounding us! Pounding us!
There is no escape!

My mask is tight,
The same air I breathe in and out.
I feel I am suffocating.
Am I dying?

**Jaspreet Binning (14)**
**Regents Park Girls' School**

# I Can Hear Them, I Can See them . . . I Can See Them

I can still hear them now,
The explosions,
The crashes,
The bombs falling from the darkened sky,
The roars and thunder,
The pounding and crushing
As the earth burst.

I can still see them now,
The daggers of flame,
The surging sea,
The graves and coffins, all destroyed.
The darkness and black,
The clouds and rain,
As the gas kills.

I can still see them now,
The casualties,
The injured,
The soldiers lying there helplessly,
The groans and moans,
The cries of pain
As the men die.

I can hear them.
I can see them . . .
I can see them.

**Rachel Tutte  (13)**
**Regents Park Girls' School**

# Messed-Up Love

Broken rib,
Bruised face,
Gotta get out,
Gotta leave this evil place.

Danger, danger, danger,
All I see is red.
Gotta get out
Before I end up dead.

I love him,
But I also feel hate.
Gotta get out
Before it's too late.

I've gotta leave home,
I've gotta leave him,
Gotta get out,
Gotta save my every limb.

Where to go?
Who to tell?
Gotta get out,
Gotta get out of hell!

He came in,
I tried to flee,
Tried to get out,
That was the end of me.

**Victoria Rothery  (12)**
**Regents Park Girls' School**

# War, War, War

'Gas, gas, gas, quick boys.'
I heard this coming from one of the trenches.
Everyone grabbed their gas masks.
A rage of fire headed our way,
People terrified, started to panic.
I managed to calm them down,
It was kind of scary, it had all gone too quiet.
Then *bang!* An explosion had hit the battleground.
We started to take cover,
It seemed like we were stuck in the trench.
A strong aroma of gas filled the muddy trench.
A man in the corner of the trench
Started to react to the gas badly, and fainted.
I acted and checked to hear a pulse.
I found it. I heard a faint call in the distance,
I couldn't see clearly, the trench was a zone of mist.
It shouted louder, 'We're under attack.'
I managed to hear. I felt sick with worry.
The soldiers' faces were unforgettable,
They all looked so tired, so fed up, so ill.
We fought back with the weapons we'd got.
It was hard, we were all so exhausted, it was impossible.
Suddenly the battlefield went quiet.
It was over.
I was so happy, yet so sad,
My body was filled with mixed emotions.
We trudged back slowly, feeling relieved.

**Carly Glasspool (13)**
**Regents Park Girls' School**

# The War To End All Wars

My wounds are as deep as a well.
I close my eyes as I try and sleep
And see the replay of every second of the day.
*Boom,* that's another dead,
The loss of an innocent life,
That person was loved as a son, a husband, a dad,
Just like that, one bullet.

They say this is the war to end all wars,
It's sweet and glorious to die for your country.
What do they know?
Nothing.
The horrors I go through *every day,*
Seeing my best friends die,
And having to fling them off that rickety wagon.
But I know, deep down,
Their souls are at home with their families,
Safe.

**Kathryn Coady  (13)**
**Regents Park Girls' School**


# Shadows In The Dark

The mists of darkness come rolling down,
The moon's silver light bathes the ground,
And where the soft light does not fall,
Creatures lurk, shadows all.

Broken branches grasp at the stars,
Pinpricks of white in the vast blackness,
Reminders of the world of light.

A harsh wind howls and screams as it blows,
Creatures of the day cower as cold fear grows,
Until the shadows that pace the night
Are banished by the morning light.

**Lizzy McKenzie  (12)**
**Regents Park Girls' School**

# The Battle

I can hear the bells,
Worried, warning bells.
Shouting, men calling,
Men with stuttering voices stop,
Then the ground stays still,
Just the echoed breathing
And the fear carries on.

I can feel the harsh goggles,
A heavy weight with a thousand straps,
My breath gets hot, steams up the mask
As I hopelessly struggle to inhale.

I can taste the same coarse breath
In my cold, leathery mask.
Every time I breathe in, the air gets hotter,
It goes down my throat
To my tight lungs, being twisted and
Twisted until there's nothing left.

I can smell rotting flesh such as
You could never imagine,
And the foul stench of sweat
From unbathed men, hard in battle,
Nervous of dying, nervous of staying alive.
A mixture of blood and vomit fills the air
Taking over your body, suffocating,
But worse, worst of all I can see,
See the coffins with the corpses which
We shall soon clone, the blinding gas
Stinging your bloodshot eyes,
As if your naked eyes are being stabbed.
Abandoned weapons never to be seen
Again by their owners.
Explosions continuously killing your friends.
Blood is drowning us. A man's leg lays
On the ground and wounded men everywhere.
Screams of pain, exhaustion and misery.
I hate this, you can almost see our souls
Leaving us right now.

How could it get like this?
Why did this have to happen to us?
But it should soon be over,
I can't last much longer.

**Sophie Freeman  (13)**
**Regents Park Girls' School**


# What A Waste Of Life

A booming blast of thunder,
An unexpected flash of lightning,
I cover my ears,
It's all so frightening.

I'm enveloped in darkness,
When someone starts to shoot.
Agony races through my veins
As I stumble and lose my boot.

I lie there, silent and motionless,
Thinking of my wife,
These could be my last moments,
What a waste of life.

What happened to the glory?
Where's all the fame?
If only I had realised
That war is such a terrible game.

**Stephanie Millard  (13)**
**Regents Park Girls' School**

# Killed For Doing Nothing

I see that the bullies have grown,
No more crude, solid fists though.
Instead, bombs have blown
Their enemies apart.

America against Iraq against Britain against who next?
Unaware of the locals,
Left confused and vexed,
'What's going on here?'

We laugh at the idea of peace now
As we watch another alien soldier wipe
The corpse's spattered blood from its brow.
Some day we will wipe its own blood from ourselves.

Forgive and forget, the stupid will say,
As our loved ones lie feeding the worms beneath.
We'll live on to fight another day,
But the grudge is in our hearts.

The cowardly scum that killed my sibling
Could only face him shielded with a rifle.
I'll use that idiot's bones for kindling
One day. Then my brother's spirit shall be appeased.

But it will not bring him back to us.
Others preach that the soldier was only following orders,
Doing as his comrades and officer do,
But how can that be true?

For who would love a murderer with cold blood?
Who could love a mindless assassin, in his heart
Is nothing, and in his soul is foul, dirty mud.
That soldier was not human to kill.

And what have we done to deserve this?
The howling heartbreak and bitter sorrow,
The icy, yet burning, kiss of death,
Our enemy's general who laughs at our tears.

Yes, what do we do that infuriates them so?
We do not comply with their rules,
We do not do as their cringing people do.
We refused to give them the country's oil . . .

And they erupt in accusing lies directed at the leader:
'You have WMD! You will kill us all!'
But he is individual, his soul alone is he the feeder,
We do not account for him. Go bully him only.

Leave us alone in our villages, leave alone the innocent,
Half of us know nothing about this politics maelstrom,
Yet our country's reputation you spitefully dent.
Now the world hates us, those who did nothing.

**Rebecca Tsao  (13)**
**Regents Park Girls' School**

# The Great War

Trudging through the muddy, bloodstained plains
Tired, aching, exhausted,
*What are we doing here?* We ask ourselves again.
No smiles, no laughter, once happy faces now contorted.

Heads drop, arms are limp, legs numb, no talking,
Injuries to the thousands, aching backs and sore feet,
Absent-minded soldiers still silently walking,
Wishing they could retreat.

In a stranger's hands, our fate lies,
Forever having to wait.
Happiness, cheerfulness, merriness dies;
Sad thoughts left on which to contemplate.

Building trenches, the only option left to take,
With the injuries and pain. Men crying.
The decision of war and fighting not theirs to make,
Over the top, guns shooting, dying.

**Sarah Machin  (13)**
**Regents Park Girls' School**

# Question Of Fear

Does it happen to anyone else?
Guess it's kind of normal.
Though why is it, it seems like it just happens to me?
Guess I'm special.
I wonder whether every day I will feel fear?
Guess it could stop.
I *want* it to stop.
Though will it?

Will I ever be left alone?
I hope so.
Is it right or wrong, what's happening to me?
I wish I knew.
Is it possible for me to tell someone?
Tell who?
*They'll* find out.
It would get worse.
*They* said so.

But what if I can't cope for any longer?
What do I do then?
Do I run? Do I hide? What?
But *they'll* find me; hunt me down, won't they?
Is there a better place?
A place where I could be left alone to share my secrets with?
Will I ever have enough money to buy *myself* some sweets?
Or at least a lunch?
No!
I won't!

Escaping such a torture
Will always seem impossible.
Getting away from all the cuts and bruises,
This will be a task.
But *if* I do escape, where would I go?
Who could I turn to?
Will I leave behind the pain and fear?
Will I carry the memory?
*Even* when they're gone?

**Kelly Bailey (14)**
**Regents Park Girls' School**

# The Atmosphere Of War

The zone of mist,
The swells and roars of thunder,
The clouds of flame,
The shells begin to hiss.

When the fields are flat,
The only other cover is the graveyard mounds.
Stumbling, treading with giant strides,
Sudden shock realises there is no escape.

Not a moment too soon,
Flames of the explosions light up the graveyard,
Surging sea, daggers of flame leap up like fountains,
The earth bursts before us.

Pounded, crushed, torn to pieces, blast in my ears,
A smack, but no pain as I sink down in the black broth,
I merely crawl still further under the coffin.
Death himself lies in it.

**Kristina Moore (13)**
**Regents Park Girls' School**


# Thoughts Of War

Darkness and doom,
Never-ending sorrow,
Hoping this war will be ending tomorrow.

Scared, watching helpless, as soldiers die.
Tears trickle from my eyes,
Wondering if I will ever survive.

Bombs and firing darken the sky,
Raging thoughts of anger,
*Why? Why?*

Keeping up spirits is all I can do,
Fighting for my country, it is my honour.
Looking to the future and thinking of you
Keeps me sane hour by hour.

**Jennifer Platt (13)**
**Regents Park Girls' School**

# War Poem

Another bomb has just exploded.
I fall, head in my hands,
Trying to forget, trying to remember.
I open my eyes, I see these ruined lands.

The lights have blinded me,
This is all too much,
It is torturing my mind.
There is something there; I dare not touch.

I get up on my feet.
In front is a man,
Should I go help him?
I don't know if I can.

I gather up my courage,
Pull him to his feet,
He is already dead,
Thrown into the wagon to take his fateful seat.

**Ami Smallwood  (14)**
**Regents Park Girls' School**


# The Hidden Talent

In the morning, a bleary figure
Hidden under the covers of his lair,
As motionless as a stone gargoyle.

At lunch, a forgotten monument,
Waiting for his comrades,
A bizarre waiter.

In art, a unique and creative creature,
A flare,
And all observers may only stare.

**Sam Matlock  (11)**
**Ryde Senior School**

# The Hidden Talent

In football, he stands motionless, unconcerned
by the cries and shouts of his fellow players.
Balls come to him and bounce off,
dimly registered from behind a gauze curtain.
He is unaffected by the fact that he has handed
the opposition the ball, just continues to watch the result.

During maths homework, he tries to concentrate,
does a few sums and loses interest, his attention
somewhere other than the continuous list of questions saying,
'Sort this information into a tally chart,
make a bar chart to show the results'.
There's only so many times you can do that while retaining interest!

In ICT, he is enveloped by his own work,
his hands flickering over the keyboard, deftly solving
any problem computer or teacher cares to throw at him,
unchallenged by other's problems,
hardly ever faltering in his work.

**Edward Stanford-Clark  (11)**
**Ryde Senior School**


# A Hidden Talent

In geography,
Her brain is a sieve.
The information goes in one ear and out the other.
She thinks it is pointless;
Why should she know that Madrid is the capital of Spain?
She is incapable of such things.

On the surfboard,
A big wave comes.
She paddles away from the monstrous
Mound of water, like a knife through butter.
The wave catches her in its grasp.
She is up, soaring on the huge wave.
This is her hidden talent.

**Alexa Boswell  (11)**
**Ryde Senior School**

# Kennings

*The Mysterious Cat*
A sharp-prowler
A claw-fouler
A night-walker
A miaow-talker
A food-scoffer
A fierce-frother
A loud-hisser
A cunning-fisher
A happy-purrer

*Struck Lightning*
A fierce-attacker
A spark-cracker
A noisy-tapper
A tense-clatter
A giant-shatter
A flame-lighter
A mighty-fighter
A riot-starter
A speedy-darter.

**James Pilkington (11)**
**Ryde Senior School**


# My Talent - Trials Bike

On his trials bike he pedals off on his career,
hopping over rocks and crevices,
accelerating off to the winner's podium.

He focuses as a hungry tiger on his prey.
He is not cocky, but sure as he wheelies
magnificently on the podium.
He sees flashes of cameras picturing him
holding a cup as his future flashes before him.

**Scout Gregory (11)**
**Ryde Senior School**

# Sea State

Upward flying,
Downward crashing,
Sideward sliding,
The air thick with salt.
The sea thick with bubbles,
The yacht ploughing through it,
The water crashing down,
The barren seascape
Claiming its victim.
Howling with rage,
Singing with sadness,
What's left behind
All but forgotten.

Warm blue seas,
Swimming with dolphins,
Silvery beaches covered in shells,
Multicoloured fish,
Swimming Neptune's expanse,
Veering and diving,
Diving and avoiding.
Blue, blue skies,
Light, wispy clouds,
What's left behind,
Forgotten.

**Mark Lewis  (14)**
**Ryde Senior School**


# Kennings - Window

A transparent version of life,
A rain's opposite defence,
A door for flowing air,
A heats goalkeeper,
An eye's block of nature,
A fragile breaker.

**Elliot Thompson  (12)**
**Ryde Senior School**

# Kennings

A hand sucker
A hard kicker
A bleating noise
A milk drinker
A dreamy sleeper
A vegetarian's darkness

A wall climber
A dew collector
A silk weaver
A dirt enterprise
A thing for a duster
A frightening phobia

A programme holder
An Internet explorer
A big button pusher
A noise buzzer
A good printer
A work saver
A new technology

A good connection
A call receiver
A button holder
A long tether
An ear listener
A voice speaker.

**Lizzy Lovegrove  (11)**
**Ryde Senior School**

# The Hidden Talent

In cross-country she stumbles along the ground gasping for breath,
the thirst stabbing at her throat like needles.

She finishes last and collapses on the ground,
like bricks stacked with no cement.

On the piano, her fingers flow across the keys,
like leaves drifting in the wind.

On the slopes, she glides down the snow,
turning the corners gracefully, avoiding other skiers.

**Katherine Dixey  (11)**
**Ryde Senior School**


# The Kiwi

Like a furry animal the kiwi sits, motionless,
Prey waiting for the pounce,
Its brown camouflage protecting its alien flesh.

Soon its hourless waiting is done,
Its humble body split in two,
The juicy green centre, oozing.

Gathered round its firm centre,
The black seeds of life fan out artistically,
Adding a crunch and texture to the succulent flesh.

The first burst of flavour,
Like a ray of the sun,
Sweet, sour, succulent or solid.

And then the kiwi is no more,
No traces but the empty fur,
The spoon, the plate, the knife.

**Alice Owen  (13)**
**St Anne's Convent School for Girls, Southampton**

# Her Name Is Lucy

Her name is Lucy,
My best friend,
Who I have a bond with,
A bond that no one can break,
A bond like a thick, twisted rope,
Just as strong, just as tight, just as close,
I have this bond with my best friend,
And her name is Lucy.

Her name is Lucy,
My best friend,
Who I am very close to,
As close as one particle of her hair to another,
So close that we're unbreakable,
Close in happiness, close in friendship, close with trust,
I am very close to my best friend,
And her name is Lucy.

Her name is Lucy,
My best friend,
Who I trust in,
I trust in her like I do the ground not to drop me,
I trust in her so much that I would not dare to break her trust,
I trust in her, I am very close to her, I have a bond with her,
I really like my best friend,
And her name is Lucy.

**Jayne Stephens (12)**
**St Anne's Convent School for Girls, Southampton**

# The Blaze

'Goodnight, sleep well!' my daddy whispers
The duvet snug around my chest
I curl myself into a ball - and sleep.

I dream of fairies, pretty princesses
Of candyfloss and daisies white
But then I hear a piercing shriek - and wake.

I sit up straight and plug my ears
The wailing screech goes on and on
I climb out of my cosy bed - to see.

A nasty smell is in the air
I can't see well for greyish fog
I open my door to take a peek - and scream.

A wall of flame flares up outside
A blaze of heat surrounds me
I cough from all the soot and ash - I cry.

I'm trapped, there's no way out at all -
The stairs are blocked with roaring flames
I need some help, I'm desperate now - I yell.

The tongues of fire are licking, creeping
Even closer to me now
I'm sweating hard from heat and fear - what now?

But then - a motion on the stairs!
The sound of hoses spraying hard!
A fount of hope springs from my heart - I'm saved!

And all at once I'm lifted high
By big, strong men in uniform
I'm carried down the stairs and out - at last.

And finally, I see my dad!
He runs to me and hugs me tight
He tells me I'm his special girl - I smile.

**Lucy Payne  (12)**
**St Anne's Convent School for Girls, Southampton**

# My Lovely Gran

My gran sits in an armchair all day,
in an ugly, slouched kind of way.
Her legs are thin,
her nose is fat,
and her voice is like a screeching cat!

She peers at you through squinted eyes,
and always knows when you've told lies.
She wears red gloves,
and woollen hat,
and is terribly fond of her scabby rat.

She dribbles in her cup of tea,
and slobbers when she kisses me.
Her breath, it smells,
her teeth are brown,
she waves goodbye and slumps back down.

**Briony Horner  (11)**
**St Anne's Convent School for Girls, Southampton**

# Ode To Chocolate Buttons

Small and round in a purple pack,
Ode to chocolate buttons in a multisack.

Cold from the fridge, or warm from the side,
Hot from your pocket where they normally hide.

Shove them in whole in your mouth in a bunch,
For breakfast or find them in your packed lunch.

You could eat them slowly, or one at a time,
Eat them however, but friend, heed this rhyme.

When you reach the last couple, don't eat them fast,
Cos all too soon you'll get to the last.

And then when you have none left to savour,
You're already missing that melt mellow flavour.

And then when you take another pack out,
Your family run after you with a shout!

**Rachel Guyer  (12)**
**St Anne's Convent School for Girls, Southampton**


# Red

The sun is like a red-hot flame,
The planet Mars is like bright red strawberries,
Your cheeks when you're embarrassed are like a rose,
Your eyes are like red apples when you're annoyed.

It means love; everyone has it in them,
Everyone's the same inside; everyone has red blood,
Red walks through the night stabbing people,
Red slips through the house without you knowing.

Red is the symbol for hot,
Red is the symbol for danger,
Red is the symbol for death,
Watch out! Is red behind you?

**Max Sampson  (13)**
**Swanmore Middle School**

# Mr Potato

They come in weird shapes and sizes and sometimes
Come out with some very big surprises!
So show some respect for Mr Potato Head
Because you can . . .
Print with 'em,
Race 'em
Electro 'em
Fire 'em
Plant 'em
Grate 'em
Chip 'em
Fry 'em
Mash 'em
Grill 'em
Micro 'em
Boil 'em
Dip 'em
Roast 'em
Crisp 'em
Stew 'em
And eat 'em!

**Warren Henley-Hunter (12)**
**Swanmore Middle School**


# What Is Green?

What is green?
Green is a big bunch of leaves just fallen from its tree,
still alive, being pushed by a slight breeze without ease.
Green is also a garden fresh with morning dew,
and with a slight whip of air, the dew splashes on the new birth of soil.
Green can also be ivy slowly climbing up an old brick wall,
as each day goes by, climbing higher and higher.
Green is Christmas, Christmas is green with Brussels sprouts.
With Christmas comes love and joy
and under a tree comes lots of toys.

**Scott Benson (12)**
**Swanmore Middle School**

# Blue

Blue is a winter breeze when you get up in the morning,
when you stretch and start yawning.
Blue is when you are feeling down,
you start to frown.
It's the colour of the sky
when you look up at the daytime.
It's the icicles in caves,
that you see at the cinema on a winter's day.
It's the wolves at night,
when they howl and fight.

When you come home on a cold day, most weeks,
blue is the colour of your cheeks.
It is the colour of the sea too,
the waves breaking that is blue.
In the night when you have a dream,
blue is that shininess, that beautiful gleam.
Blue is when you're at the door,
when you can't stand that coldness any more.
Blue is also when you say goodbye,
to someone you love, it's the feeling inside.
To me, to you,
everything can be blue.

**Jak Downing  (12)**
**Swanmore Middle School**


# Pink

Pink is a beautiful and a wonderful colour,
Pink is skin which looks as pink as a pink Porky Pig,
Pink is a rose which lightens the garden with its lovely pink
                                petals flowing through the air,
Pink is a lipgloss; sparkling, glittery gloss,
Pink is a beautiful teddy as soft as a cloud in the sky,
Pink is a big, round lollipop to make your tongue to bright pink,
Pink is a girl with a very pink dress,
Pink is the air smelling of lavender through the sky.

**Tara Hayward  (12)**
**Swanmore Middle School**

# My Strawberry Poem

S trawberries, Sadie's favourite fruit.
T ravelling or sitting down.
R osy-red and ripe.
A t home or round the town.
W ith lots of cream and sugar.
B ig and very juicy.
E very mouthful a delight.
R idiculously tasty.
R eally, really scrumptious.
Y ummy, yummy, really scrummy.

**Sadie McLean  (12)**
**Swanmore Middle School**


# Blue

Cold is the blue at the night,
Blue is the line of piercing light,
Blue is a wolf darting through the snow,
Blue is a bluebell blowing slow,
Blue is the eyes following you around the room,
Blue icicles fall with a boom,
Bluebird singing on the wall,
The sky when all the clouds fall,
Blue ink all over a book,
The sea glistens when you take a look.

**Josh Goddard  (12)**
**Swanmore Middle School**

# What Is Pink?

Pink, pink is the colour of a rose,
Pink is the colour of a cold nose,
Pink is a colour that makes you feel happy,
But sometimes it makes you feel a bit snappy,
Pink is the colour of my favourite jam,
It is also the colour of some ham,
Pink is the colour of your rosy cheeks,
Pink is the colour of some rock chick's streaks,
Pink is the colour of my folder,
You may not like it when you get older,
Pink is the colour of my grandad's hand,
And is also the colour of my favourite hairband.

**Christie Smith (12)**
**Swanmore Middle School**


# Silver

Silver is a starry midnight sky
And the wings of a beautiful insect
It's the trail of snails
On all the walls
The sky when a storm fails
It's the glisten on a wet window sill
When the rain falls
We all love silver upon a Christmas tree
The sparkle on the waves
It's the colour we always see.

**Rachael Wade (12)**
**Swanmore Middle School**

# Black And White

Black is the night that hugs the land,
White is the sunshine that breaks the darkness,
Black is the winter, all bitter and cold,
White is that first flower of spring,
Black is the hatred, lies and deceit,
White is the love that sweeps you off your feet,
Black is the evil that consumes that heart,
White is the good that shines like a candle,
Black is Hell, full of horror and pain,
White is Heaven, full of laughter and light,
Black is the guilt bubbling up inside,
White is not telling a single lie.

We all want to be like the colour white, but really we're all grey.

**Bryony Morey  (13)**
**Swanmore Middle School**


# Red

Red is anger building up inside someone,
Red is fire burning and crackling through the night,
Red is running through the night murdering as it goes.

Red is the planet Mars floating in space,
Red is a girl's rosy cheeks when she comes in from the cold,
Red is a poppy swaying in the cold breeze.

Red is a man's back after sitting in the sun for too long.
Red is a rose growing silently in the garden,
Red is a lady's bright lipstick glistening in the moonlight.

**Chloe Shelford  (12)**
**Swanmore Middle School**

# My Purple Poem

P olish glistening on my nails in the sun.
U mbrellas bright and colourful.
R elaxing lavender sticks.
P arma Violets are delicious.
L etting Dairy Milk melt on your tongue.
E eyore, his soft, cuddly tummy.

**Stacy van Meerkerk  (12)**
**Swanmore Middle School**


# He

She felt death itself
Tap her on her tense shoulder,
It darkened her screams.

The screams fill the air,
Piercing like a carving knife,
Floating down the hall.

Hiding in the room,
His eyes staring, tail flicking,
Cleaning his whiskers.

Stands 'round the corner,
Knife clasped in his splintered paws,
Dives for his victim.

First his claw tightens,
Choking her, stealing her soul,
He drops her body.

His shadow dies down,
Soaking into the carpet
Like his victim's blood.

**Cathryn Jordan  (11)**
**The Bourne Community College**

# The Terrible Noise!

Have you heard the tale of the girls and boys
Who woke the dead with their terrible noise?
A more frightful thing has never been seen,
Than this on the night of that Hallowe'en.

The ghosts and the witches come out to play,
And boys and girls lie and play with the dead.
A more frightful thing has never been seen,
Than this on the night of that Hallowe'en.

The pumpkins glow as the shadows go by,
As they cry, they think that they might die.
A more frightful thing has never been seen,
Than this on the night of that Hallowe'en.

Nobody dared to go out
With all the witches and ghosts about.
A more frightful thing has never been seen,
Than this on the night of that Hallowe'en.

He snuck 'round the street
And the witches and ghosts he did meet.
A more frightful thing has never been seen,
Than this on the night of that Hallowe'en.

They said they would never ever dare,
To go, at Hallowe'en, out there!
A more frightful thing has never been seen,
Than this on the night of that Hallowe'en.

This is a warning to all who dare,
Of witches and ghouls you must beware.
A more frightful thing has never been seen,
Than this on the night of that Hallowe'en.

**Charlotte Thomas  (11)**
**The Bourne Community College**

# Have You Heard?

Have you heard the tale of the girls and boys,
Who woke the dead with their terrible noise?
A more frightful thing has never been seen,
Than this on the night of that Hallowe'en.

The spirit and the madness,
With scary old witches.
A more frightful thing has never been seen,
Than this on the night of that Hallowe'en.

Down in the woods where the werewolves came,
Their souls were all the same.
A more frightful thing has never been seen,
Than this on the night of that Hallowe'en.

In the icy potholes,
Where the head of a spirit lies.
A more frightful thing has never been seen,
Than this on the night of that Hallowe'en.

Have you seen the boys
With the frightful thrills and chills?
A more frightful thing has never been seen,
Than this on the night of that Hallowe'en.

Have you seen the forests where the phantoms lie,
Undead but still alive?
A more frightful thing has never been seen,
Than this on the night of that Hallowe'en.

This is a warning to all who dare,
Of witches and ghouls you must beware.
A more frightful thing has never been seen,
Than this on the night of that Hallowe'en.

**Eleanor Heaton  (11)**
**The Bourne Community College**

# On This Haunting Night Of Hallowe'en

The chills of the undead's spirit
Reach out into the werewolf's mind.
Madness cries out from the phantom's soul
And the witch's icy head dies.
A zombie splinters and thrills
As it smashes and shreds through
The old, creaky cabin.
The pumpkins eat flesh and blood
On this haunting night of Hallowe'en.

**Tom Portsmouth  (12)**
**The Bourne Community College**

# The Bloody Lady Haiku

A lady of death.
The blood running down my back.
My skin burns with fright.

**Jasmin Jackson  (12)**
**The Bourne Community College**

# The Key

The thing that bothers me the most
Is when they stick me in the keyhole.
They turn me round and make me dizzy
And then hang me upside down,
I spin for half an hour.
Then they throw me on the sofa,
I fall down the back of the cushions
And they can't find me for two weeks.

**Owen Tomsett  (12)**
**The Bourne Community College**

# The Paperclip

I hate those humans!
Always bending me to be used to pick locks.
How would they like to be bent
And used to pick locks, hah?
How come I'm silver
And the others are multicoloured?
How would they feel
If they were the odd one out?

**Ryan Hillier (11)**
**The Bourne Community College**

# Scary Senses Haiku

Rats scuttled past me,
Had chills growing down my back.
I could smell stale sweat.

**Luke Edwards (11)**
**The Bourne Community College**

# Hallowe'en

Icy breath
As madness death.

Witch's cries
When werewolf dies.

Phantom splinters
With madness fingers.

Spirit souls
With deadly ghouls.

**Bradley Lock (11)**
**The Bourne Community College**

# As

As dull as a Goth,
Mouth like a burger bun,
As freaky as a haunted house.
Loud like a heartbeat
With a stethoscope on it.
As large as a bear,
Smelly like a boy's socks.
As realistic as a French lesson.
Skin like a vampire in a mirror.
As dead as a graveyard.
Guts oozing out like pus in a spot.
As terrifying as a werewolf,
Eyes like red lasers.

**Courtney Brannigan (11)**
**The Bourne Community College**


# The Penny

Here we go again . . .
always being put in the wash,
being in smelly pockets,
in machines,
left under the couch,
thrown away,
flattened,
given to other people.

See how they like it being a penny.
Put in the wash,
flattened,
in machines.
See how they like being me, one day.

**Nicole Stubbs (11)**
**The Bourne Community College**

# Hallowe'en's Ballad

Have you heard the tale of the girls and boys,
Who woke the dead with their terrible noise?
A more frightful thing has never been seen,
Than this on the night of that Hallowe'en.

The table fell down, guts came out
And ate it like chewing gum.
A more frightful thing has never been seen,
Than this on the night of that Hallowe'en.

The disgusting zombies came out of the grave,
They danced around the tombs and had a rave.
A more frightful thing has never been seen,
Than this on the night of that Hallowe'en.

Big, hairy spiders came out at midnight,
They attacked the children and gave them a fright.
A more frightful thing has never been seen,
Than this on the night of that Hallowe'en.

Belly dropped down, head came out,
Then there was heard a bloodcurdling shout!
A more frightful thing has never been seen,
Than this on the night of that Hallowe'en.

Witches all busy making spells to cast,
To take the children back to the past.
A more frightful thing has never been seen,
Than this on the night of that Hallowe'en.

This is a warning to all who dare,
Of witches and ghouls you must beware.
A more frightful thing has never been seen,
Than this on the night of that Hallowe'en.

**Stacie Biggs (12)**
**The Bourne Community College**

# The Spoon

Excuse me if I moan a little,
but I'm so fed up
with people shoving me into their mouths!
And I'm also fed up because they
use my head.
Yeah, that's right!
To bash me around their cups!
I've had enough of being scorched by
their precious tea.

I would just love it
if I used their heads to
bash them
about in the cup
and shove them into mouths!

**Peter Rogers (11)**
**The Bourne Community College**


# Don't Go Out This Hallowe'en

The linger of death
And the cries of the undead
Haunt my dreams tonight.

I hear the witch cry
As the knife pierces her white skin.
I sit listening.

Beware of the moan
Of the deadly mobile phone.
You can't go to sleep.

You knock on the door,
It creaks open, you are shot
*Dead* with a shotgun.

**Ellie Williams (11)**
**The Bourne Community College**

# Rubber Gloves

I hate my life as a rubber glove!
The smells,
the sights,
I hate it all!
When I think where I've been,
it sends shivers down my rubber fingers.

I also hate the smell of bleach,
especially close up.
It's worse than the smell 'before'.

People think they can put their hands anywhere
just because they have got me on,
but it's not going to happen anymore!

Many times I have been lowered into the toilet
of doom,
but tomorrow I will refuse,
and seek my revenge on them!

**Harriet Weetman  (11)**
**The Bourne Community College**


# My First Day At School

My knees were knocking,
My voice was quaking,
The clocks were ticking,
My hand was aching.

Some people tall,
Some teachers cruel,
But most were cool,
And I felt small.

I had heard that people were mean,
But that was not the way it seemed.
But overall, I thought this school
Was the coolest of them all.

**Sadie Prior  (12)**
**The Bourne Community College**

# Simile Song

A ghost jumps out,
As white as snow,
An eerie chill
Fills the room,
Oh no!

A full moon at the dead of night,
Werewolf tail, fluffy as a duster,
Yellow teeth to give you a bite.
Once it's got the taste of blood
There's no hope,
It goes to its next victim.

Eyeballs pop
Like balloons when they meet a pin.
Blood oozes, *slip, slop, slap.*
A monster comes with a big grin,
Teeth as big as a head,
You can't tackle it, it will win!

**Ann-Marie Wood  (11)**
**The Bourne Community College**

# Cackle!

I could hear the cackle
Of witches,
The howling and
Crunching of werewolves.
The death-like spirits,
Raising the cries and the thrills
From children.

I went downstairs
To find living dead.
I found it hard to breathe,
In - out,
I said to myself, 'Madness,
The whole thing, Hallowe'en.'

**Joe Nieddu  (11)**
**The Bourne Community College**

# Watch Out!

Watch out when you are about,
You might find a head eating a sprout.
A more frightful thing has never been seen,
Than this on the night of that Hallowe'en.

You might see guts hanging around,
Because the butcher butchered for a pound.
A more frightful thing has never been seen,
Than this on the night of that Hallowe'en.

The guts hit the fan,
Like some jam.
A more frightful thing has never been seen,
Than this on the night of that Hallowe'en.

**Jay Rhodes (11)**
**The Bourne Community College**


# What Am I?

Mouths, mouths, mouths!
That's all I ever get.
I'm always getting dribbled on,
I'm always getting drooled on.
First of all I'm clean
And then I'm soaking wet!

**Georgette Kramer (11)**
**The Bourne Community College**


# The Doughnut

I hate being bitten a little to find the jam.
Then they lick my blood out of my stomach.
I really hate it when they bite me
And the jam spurts out at the edge.
The icing crunches like it's my bones.

**Gregg Turner (11)**
**The Bourne Community College**

# Hallowe'en Ballad

Have you heard the tale of the girls and boys
Who woke the dead with their terrible noise?
A more frightful thing has never been seen,
Than this on the night of that Hallowe'en.

Oozing guts and bleeding spleens,
All mushed up like mushy beans.
A more frightful thing has never been seen,
Than this on the night of that Hallowe'en.

Grim Reaper comes to play,
All the kids run away.
A more frightful thing has never been seen,
Than this on the night of that Hallowe'en.

Haunted houses everywhere,
Ghosts come out and give a scare.
A more frightful thing has never been seen,
Than this on the night of that Hallowe'en.

The madness of the undead shred,
And once a year their brains go dead.
A more frightful thing has never been seen,
Than this on the night of that Hallowe'en.

Zombies are alive, ready to go,
Let's run away and stay low.
A more frightful thing has never been seen,
Than this on the night of that Hallowe'en.

This is a warning to all who dare,
Of witches and ghouls you must beware.
A more frightful thing has never been seen,
Than this on the night of that Hallowe'en.

**Marc Noble (11)**
**The Bourne Community College**

# The Body!

Blood ran down the door
As a body lay on the floor.
A more frightful thing has never been seen,
Than this on the night of that Hallowe'en.

Candy on the doormat,
Soon replaced with the remains of his hat.
A more frightful thing has never been seen,
Than this on the night of that Hallowe'en.

The lamp post was gone,
Or was it a con?
A more frightful thing has never been seen,
Than this on the night of that Hallowe'en.

**Megan Grant (11)**
**The Bourne Community College**


# The Paintbrush

Light and dark colours,
rainbow colours more,
my paintbrush is used in them all.

First the paintbrush
is swished
and swirled
in cold, wet water.
Yellow, purple, red and blue,
my paintbrush is ready to be dipped in you.

Finished painting for today,
bristles cleaned and dried.
Brushes put away
for another day.

**Steven Peterson (11)**
**The Bourne Community College**

## Scary Simile Song

As scary as a tarantula,
As monstrous as a witch.
Deadly like a potion,
Like a ghostly howl in the wind.

The phantom cries,
This is like madness.
A ball rolls like a revolting head,
Undead like a hideous pumpkin.

Like a mummy's deep breath,
As a phantom scream,
Like a cat.
The English teacher cackles like a witch.

**Jade Gunn  (11)**
**The Bourne Community College**


## Spinner Top

Spinning around, spinning around,
I'm getting dizzy, spinning around.
All the people are having fun,
While I hate getting dizzy, spinning around.
Getting bruised,
Getting battered,
My paintwork getting chipped.
I hate all the people who keep
Spinning me around.

Izzy whizzy, I get dizzy,
Spinning 'round and 'round.
When I stop I have to drop,
And fall onto the ground.

**Gavin Fewell  (11)**
**The Bourne Community College**

# Hallowe'en Spills

Hallowe'en thrills give me chills,
My sadness equals madness,
There's a hole that takes your soul,
The phantoms give me tantrums,
The witches make cries from the sky.

**Luke Ayling  (11)**
**The Bourne Community College**


# Holidays

If you want a holiday in the sun
you'll surely want to have some fun.

When you play with the sand
you feel like you are on an island

The happy times in the sea
with the family and me.

If you are feeling hot
try and drink a lot

Lying in the summer heat
thinking about what to eat

Many people swim in the pool
to try and keep themselves cool

Feeling all that summer joy
is like getting a new toy

Have a good time spending your money
even if it is on something funny

Playing with my bucket and spade
and everyone looking at what I've made.

**Abigail-Jade Westerman Harris  (12)**
**The Sholing Technology College**

# When I Grow Up!

When I grow up I want to be like my sister,
Go clubbing, wear hot clothes and high heels
And make my friends jealous,
I would dance all night.
I can't wait to go to the prom,
Go in limos and dance with boys,
That's what I dream of,

Get a job and be working all day,
Hard work though,
Get married and have children,
That's what I would like,

Go to Disney World with the kids,
Go on rides and have so much fun,
Have birthdays, get older and older each year,
I'll try and be a good mum through all of the years,
I will stay so happy and live my life till the end,
Till the very end,
Babysit the grandchildren,

Growing up will be so much fun,
But not as much as being young.

**Brittania Stokes  (12)**
**The Sholing Technology College**


# New World

I stand alone at the gate of this new world,
A fresh book, a new leaf, it's all the same in this big world,
I walk in not saying a word,
It's big and scary in this strange world.
Everything harder, newer, bigger, in this odd world,
I feel young yet older in this mad world.
I walk into a room,
I'm not alone in this new world.

**Danielle Phillips  (11)**
**The Sholing Technology College**

# I Like Penguins

I like penguins,
They're so cute,
They walk around in a black and white suit.

I like penguins,
They're so nice,
They slide around on snow and ice.

I like penguins,
They huddle together,
We all know why, because of the weather.

I like penguins,
They look like waiters,
But actually, they're good skaters.

I like penguins,
I'm sure you've guessed,
They are just the best.

**Olivia Stay  (13)**
**The Sholing Technology College**


# My Pet Hamster

I have a hamster as a pet
His name is Sidney, don't forget.
Cute and fluffy, grey and white
He keeps me awake in the night.
Running around in his wheel
After that he has his meal.
He cleans himself all the time
Running around until nine.
Sleeping all through the day
Not a peep or squeak to say!

**Jade Palmer  (12)**
**The Sholing Technology College**

# Shoes

Different colours, different sizes
Spotty, stripy, full of surprises
Sizes 1, 2, 3, or 4,
Each one will tell us more.
Small heels, high heels,
Have a pair of each,
You can wear them anywhere
Even on a beach.

Winter ones, summer ones,
Sweaty or smelly,
Pointy ones, sporty ones
Sandals or wellies.

Pink ones, blue ones,
Purple or green,
Orange and yellow,
The best we've ever seen!

**Jessica Palmer  (12)**
**The Sholing Technology College**


# Bullies

Just because I love school
doesn't make me uncool
but all the other children say
'Just take it, you're the boff of the day!'

My mother says, 'Never mind,'
but she doesn't know how it hurts inside.
I suffer in silence over what they say
I take it strongly every day!

In the end I just will say
'I'll have a better future anyway!'

**Katherine Watts  (12)**
**The Sholing Technology College**

# Poem About Blenkinsop

'Late again Blenkinsop, what's the excuse this time?'
'Not my fault, Ma'am.'
'Whose fault is it then?'
'Grandma's, Ma'am.'
'Grandma's? What did she do?'
'She . . . kind of . . . died, Ma'am.'
'Died? That makes four this term and all on PE days, Blenkinsop.'
'I know, it's very upsetting Ma'am.'
'How many grandmothers have you got?'
'None, Ma'am. All dead.'
'What about yesterday, Blenkinsop?'
'What about yesterday, Ma'am?'
'You missed maths.'
'That was the dentist.'
'The dentist?' (sarcastically)
No Ma'am, my teeth, Ma'am.'
'You missed the test.'
'I had been looking forward to it, Ma'am.'
'Right line up for PE.'
'I can't, Ma'am.'
'No such word as 'can't', why can't you?'
'No kit, Ma'am.'
'Where is it?'
'Home, Ma'am.'
'What is it doing at home?'
'Not ironed, Ma'am.'
'Why not? Who usually does it?'
'Grandma, Ma'am.'
Why couldn't she do it?'
*'Dead, Ma'am!'*

**Jaanki Patel (12)**
**The Sholing Technology College**

# My Cute Friend

Hammy the hamster is here to stay,
We loved him from the very first day,
He likes to run and roll around the floor,
But comes to a stop when he hits the door,
He loves to climb and run about,
But runs to hide when I start to shout,
He's cute and smart,
And as swift as a dart,
(Especially when racing through tubes),
He gnaws and chews, even through shoes,
Then off he goes for a snooze.

**Lucy Gray  (12)**
**The Sholing Technology College**

# Love Is . . .

Love is pure, love is gold
Love is never found cold
Love is sugar, love is sweet
Love is given like a treat.

Love is pumping, love is the heart
Love is not to be apart
Love is warm, love is red
Love is a secret not to be said.

**Pamela Barrett  (12)**
**The Sholing Technology College**

# My Pet Guppie,

Is a beautiful angelfish,
He glides through the water,
Going *swish, swish, swish.*
As he goes to sleep,
He quickly has a peep,
At the open wide world around him.

**Amy Phillips  (12)**
**The Sholing Technology College**

# Bullies

When bullies go to school,
They think they rule,
They're really mean,
They always have been.

When they go past the rusty red gates,
They run along and meet their mates,
Bullies like to get their own way,
They don't run about, jump or play.

Bullies are cruel,
They think they rule,
They think they're tough,
They're really rough.

They like to call people names and jeer,
When they go past little children they like to sneer,
Bullies are children's worst fear,
When they're alone, bullies suddenly appear.

**Shawna Metcalf  (12)**
**The Sholing Technology College**


# Alone . . .

I walk alone whilst feeling nervous,
whispers all around me.
I finally get to where it's safe.
I sit and wait.

I concentrate on important work
but it's hard to ignore the whispers.
Physical abuse begins,
bruises appear.

Work is over and done with,
I hear a loud ringing sound,
I move quickly whilst panting,
I'm safe, I'm home.

**Kelly-Ann Norris  (12)**
**The Sholing Technology College**

# The Seasons

*Spring,* makes me feel happy
When all the chocolate is sold
Because the winter has just passed
We no longer feel cold.

*Summer,* fills us all with happiness
We wear anything to keep us cool
Sometimes the heat is unbearable
We need to jump in a pool.

*Autumn,* when all the leaves are falling
And the roads are full with puddles
We need to be keeping warm
With lots of hugs and cuddles.

*Winter,* when the snowflakes are falling
And, when the snow lays
We want to go and enjoy ourselves
So we go out and play.

**Sophie-Jade Smith  (11)**
**The Sholing Technology College**

# Pink

Pink is great and pink is fine,
It's even the colour of sweet, sweet wine,
It's there to comfort you when you're down,
Out and about when you're in town.

It's all around you as you can see,
Do you like it as much as me?
Pink is the best,
It's better than all the rest,
Pink is divine,
It's mine, mine, mine.

**Laura O'Donoghue  (12)**
**The Sholing Technology College**

# Handbags

H andbags
A re useful.
N ice ones too.
D iamonds and gems.
B est for you.
A ll nice and handy.
G reat for you and me.
S o let's go on a handbag spree!

**Jade Wyse  (12)**
**The Sholing Technology College**

# Hamsters

Hamsters play in their wheel
And eat apple peel
They sleep in the day
But wake up at night to play

When they're sad
You feel so bad
Because you are their mother
Run to the pet shop and get them a brother!

**Louise Burke  (12)**
**The Sholing Technology College**

# Winter Wonders

Winter is the coldest season.
The land is covered with ice and frost.
People like to wrap up warm.
Scarves and gloves are the fashion.

Christmas time is round the corner.
Children plead for lots of presents.
Snowball fights are the game of the season.
Wintertime is so much fun.

**Erin Foster  (12)**
**The Sholing Technology College**

# Night

Some people think of night
as an event that happens after daylight.

Some people may think of it
as a kind person or a cheat.

I, for one, think of night,
as a gentle thing,
not a creature it would harm,
nope, not a thing!

Most kids say they're scared of night,
so they ask their parents for a nightlight.

Night might be something that helps us sleep,
once she does that, she relaxes her feet.

Night is my favourite time of day,
because I get to go to bed - but I should pray.

**Marelle Steblecki (11)**
**The Sholing Technology College**


# Magazines

Magazines have lots of pages
And that's how the eds get wages.
Magazines are full of laughter
While reading them and sometimes after.

Magazines are chunky, large or small
You can buy one for the school ball.
You can write to solve your problem
And dear old Deirdre will sort them.

If you don't buy a magazine you won't be
the top goss queen!

**Hannah McCormick (12)**
**The Sholing Technology College**

# Witches

When the shades of night start falling
and the sun sinks down,

Witches come swooping,
from their secret magic town.

They bring their cloaks, their hats and cats
and they fly . . .

Up and down, round and round,
over treetops, past the town.

All is dark, all is quiet,
apart from the wind and the rustling trees, *whoosh!*

Under the bridge, through the forest,
until the clock strikes one.

Then the witches fly back
to their secret magic town.

**Katherine Newman  (12)**
**The Sholing Technology College**


# Dogs

Big dogs, little dogs,
Barking really madly,
Howling at the moon,
Behaving really badly,
Chasing after cats,
Chasing after rats,
Mostly acting crazy,
But some can be lazy.
After a long day,
The noise and playing will cease,
They will be at rest,
And we will get our peace.

**Sophie-Fern Jarvis  (12)**
**The Sholing Technology College**

# Santa Claus

Santa Claus does not use doors,
He climbs right down the chimney,
He carries his sack on top of his back
And puts presents under the tree.

He eats his mince pies,
And children who lie
Don't receive a present.

On Christmas Day, people play
With their brand new toys,
And enjoy a feast that could fill a beast.

At Christmas you fill your tum
And have great fun with your family,
It's a time to share and a time to care
With the ones you love.

**Rebecca Gilbank (12)**
**The Sholing Technology College**


# Dogs

My dog is called Tilly,
She acts all silly.
She is really sweet,
But not very neat.

She chases all the cats,
But she's scared of all rats.
She is really crazy,
But sometimes she is lazy.

When she is asleep,
She doesn't make a peep.
She doesn't act like a lady,
But she's still my baby.

**Naomi Jerrim (12)**
**The Sholing Technology College**

# My Love For You

My love for you
Will fill trillions of pots
Which means I love you lots and lots.

I think of you all day and night
You are that piece of shining light.

I need you here
I need you now
You've always shown me why and how.

You've always been there for me
Through thick and through thin
You have never chucked me in the bin.

You're getting old now, you need some help
It's my turn now, Granny,

I'll be your nanny.

**Kirsty Griffin (11)**
**The Sholing Technology College**


# My Baby Cousins

My baby cousins are so sweet,
They always wriggle their two feet,
Their hair is as soft as a polar bear's coat,
Their eyes are as blue as a summer's sky,
Their little noses are as small as a little bumblebee.

My cousins make me so happy,
Every time I see them I light up with joy,
They are my little cousins,
I buy them things like teddies and rings,
Oh, how they love them!
They are my little cousins,
The best cousins in the world.

**Lauren Wing (13)**
**The Sholing Technology College**

# Dagger Death

The glittering blade,
The sharp edge.
The scraping metal,
The ivory handle.

Lifting it up,
And bringing it down.
Running away,
Not making a sound.

Wiping the blade,
And hanging it up.
Still a red stain,
On the white cloth.

Feeling the guilt,
Feeling his conscience.
Wiping his face,
Can't get to sleep.

Hiding the body,
Feeling the tension.
Driven to madness,
Seeing the ghost.

Confessing the truth,
Sitting in a cell.
Waiting for his end,
To join his dead friend.

Feeling the rope,
Around his neck.
Looking ahead sombrely,
And taking the jump.

**Elizabeth McCulloch (12)**
**The Sholing Technology College**

# Friends

I was new and you were old,
I had no friends but you were there,
You showed me round,
And became my friend,
Then you went away and then came back,
And brought me lots of presents.

I cried in your arms and you cried in mine,
You slept round my house and hugged me loads,
So I didn't feel alone.

I think it's best,
We leave each other,
To do our own little thing,
To make new friends and do our best,
So now we have been parted.

**Zoey Coyne (12)**
**The Sholing Technology College**


# Winter

Winter is here! What a charm!
The cold is not very calm
People lying in the snow
Making stars and having a go.

People here love to play
Even on a rainy day
People love having fun
Even when they're with their mums.

Snowball fights in the cold
Make people look very bold
Snowflakes falling from the sky
Now it's time to say goodbye!

**Hannah Bowler (12)**
**The Sholing Technology College**

# My Boy

This boy of mine
He's mighty fine
He makes my knees weak
When he kisses my cheek

He makes me laugh, he makes me cry
He makes me ask the question 'Why?'
Why would he go for a girl like me
I'm just an average teenage dweeb

He took me on a date
And told me he loved my mate
I fell apart
He broke my heart

My first relationship down the drain
He put me through a lot of pain
He is a loser boy
Who treated me like a toy.

**Emma Wright  (12)**
**The Sholing Technology College**


# My Heart

*(For my mum and sister, Stephanie)*

My heart is full of gold,
Like the hearts of others,
My heart is full of love,
Mine is like my mother's.

My heart doesn't just belong to me,
My family owns it too,
My heart is very special,
I need it to love you.

**Tanya Harris  (12)**
**The Sholing Technology College**

# Love

Morning comes, so tired
'You have to be up in a minute'

'Don't worry, I'll be OK'
Awakening slowly, it's too bright
'You must be ready now'

My baby cousin
So bubbly and bright
Little giggles from a little mouth
So cute and cuddly
Curled in my arms
So quiet and small
Goodnight to you all

My cousins
Look up to me
My cousins
Grow on me
My cousins
Tag along with me
My cousins
Love me.

**Abbey Gordon  (14)**
**The Sholing Technology College**


# Christmas

C  hristmas is coming.
H  olly is growing.
R  eindeer ready.
 I  n every house fires are on.
S  anta's got his belt on.
T  urkeys are all cooked.
M  erry Christmas
A  nd Santa's coming.
S  leep tight.

**Jo James  (12)**
**The Sholing Technology College**

# The Love Beneath The Sea . . .

What's down there?
A locket of love . . .
Sent from above!
An emotional sea of time . . .

How deep does it go?
Does anyone know
The truth behind the waves . . . ?

How does it feel?
The sea of blue and green,
Gold flashes from the sun
Running down a never-ending stream . . .

Love is the word,
That I know . . .
It explains all these words,
And they can all go!

**Alannah Knowles (11)**
**The Sholing Technology College**


# Hallowe'en

H allowe'en is full of excitement
A nd children waiting to call trick or treat.
L urking about the streets, knocking door to door,
L ooking for their friends with all their scary costumes.
O ver the road and everywhere people decorate their
   houses for Hallowe'en night,
W e knock on the door and say, 'Trick or treat?'
   where we're given some sweets to put in our bags.
E ating our sweets galore, we hurry home,
E veryone is now at home.
N ow wasn't that a cheerful night?

**Claire Medcalf (12)**
**The Sholing Technology College**

# Lea

My dog is so fluffy
I'm glad she's not scruffy
She doesn't ever bite
But she does tend to fight.

My uncle is called Mark,
He takes her down the park,
She likes to eat meat
But she also has treats.

**Helen Wilcox (13)**
**The Sholing Technology College**


# Christmas Time

It's Christmas time at last,
Look at the droplets on the grass,
Can you see the lights all around?
Can you see the snow on the ground?
All the children making snowmen,
All the teenagers making a den,
All the family comes together,
To celebrate their time with each other.

**Gemma Dashwood (13)**
**The Sholing Technology College**


# Half-Term!

No more school, no more work
End of school, half-term's here!
No more lessons, no more teachers
No more rules, half-term's here!
Whole week full of fun,
Going out, staying up late!
Now it's half-term, parents nagging
Can't wait to go back to school!

**Rebecca Grogan (12)**
**The Sholing Technology College**

# You Weren't There

When I came home,
You weren't there,
You didn't know,
You didn't care,

When I came home,
You weren't there,
Bags left packed,
It's not fair,

When I came home,
You weren't there,
A noise in my bedroom,
A woman there, left to care,

When I came home,
You weren't there,
You couldn't look at me straight,
Not even a stare.

**Elisha Mason  (12)**
**The Sholing Technology College**

# My Sis

Mia-Lilli at 6lbs 2
Seven months passed
How much she grew
From a helpless newborn
Her life begun
My tiny sis is so much fun
The special gift I never thought I'd get
And the love we have I'll never forget
Soon I know she'll be a tiny terror
But the memories of her as a newborn
I shall treasure forever.

**Aimee Vine  (12)**
**The Sholing Technology College**

# My Holiday In Spain!

M y first time flying with my family
Y elling, cheering, shouting 'Yippee!'

H aving fun in the clear, blue pool,
O n the beach playing volleyball.
L ying in the scorching hot sun,
I n my bikini, this is so much fun.
D ancing in the disco with my mate,
A lways exciting! Staying up late.
Y ikes! We're covered in midge bites that irritate.

I n the water park, getting wet,
N umber the slides and friends I've met.

S pain's biggest theme park! Here we come!
P icture the 10-loop roller coaster, I went on without Mum!
A ll the two weeks I really enjoyed,
I 've got to go home now, I'm really annoyed!
N ever to forget this holiday for the rest of my life.

**Danielle Lebbern (12)**
**The Sholing Technology College**


# Christmas

Mince pies are placed on the table
The cake is covered in maple
The crackers and cutlery are sorted
The Christmas tree is sparkled
The presents are in different piles
For each of the family
When it's time to open the presents
The children's faces are full of glee.

All their stomachs rumble
Wait till they have their apple crumble
Once again comes Santa Claus
His reindeer pattering their golden hooves.

**Sophie Hayter (12)**
**The Sholing Technology College**

# Me!

I look around and what do I see?
My life, my family and me.
Complicated as my life may seem,
I always find ways to make myself gleam . . .

My family, sister, Mum, Dad and me.
That's always how I want it to be.
Whether we're shouting, laughing or playing a game,
That's how I want it to stay. The same.

My friends. Bright, funny, pretty and tall,
We never argue, just laugh and I like them all.
Forever chatting, laughing and lending a hand,
And we love the chance to mess around.

So there you have it, although it's not all there,
Like idols and hobbies, I have in my head somewhere,
I love my life, my family and friends,
I really don't want this life to ever end . . .

**Louisa Osborn  (14)**
**The Sholing Technology College**


# Under The Bed

In the morning and afternoon, under the bed is how it should be.

Old clothes I forgot about; last year's Hallowe'en outfits,
dated 1971 library books.

However when I go to bed, they start their evil deeds.

The old clothes dress up as ghosts and haunt my bedroom,
next the vampire and witch from Hallowe'en outfits suck my blood;
the witch casts wicked spells, the library books hit me with
their dusty pages.

But then I open my eyes and look under the bed, it's just the same.
The old clothes, Hallowe'en outfits and the old books -
ready for tomorrow's scare.

**Alice McNamara  (11)**
**The Sholing Technology College**

# The Makeover

First on goes the foundation that spreads all round your face,
It's so runny and sticky that it goes all over the place.
Second goes the eyeliner, that goes on your eyeline,
It's like a sharp pencil I keep that's mine.
Next it's the eyeshadow, the nice sparkly stuff,
It makes you look pretty and most of all buff.
Then it's the mascara, that dresses your lashes
It's like an SOS, dots and dashes.
Now it's the blusher, that brightens up your face,
It's like a golden sun that shines all over the place.
Finally it's the lipstick, that kisses up your lips,
It's like a thick tube that looks so shiny you wanna have a kip
So that's all you need if you wanna have a makeover,
And you can put it all on in your bedroom or your sofa.

**Hayley Wells  (13)**
**The Sholing Technology College**


# My Jack Russell

I've got a Jack Russell
He's all teeth and muscle,
Those little white nippers
Disintegrate slippers,
His aim in life is to chew
By the way have you seen my left shoe?

The food that we eat
He regards as a treat,
I'm getting much thinner
Because he eats half my dinner,
So forget about your pal and chum
I wonder which one of us is dumb?

**Catherine Williams  (12)**
**The Sholing Technology College**

# Hard Times

*Hard times.* When the sound of music never plays.
*Hard times.* When the sound of children's laughter is erased.

*Hard times.* When the only song you hear is filled with
sadness and fears.
A song so cruel and terrible it could move you to tears.

*Hard times.* When the sun never seems to show its face,
or shine some light over this forgotten race.

*Hard times.* When the silence is shattered by a horrific scream,
and you're sitting there crying, praying it was
just a dream.

*Hard times.* When the tears never seem to stop falling from your
eyes, or when all the happiness seems to be replaced by
many sorrowful cries.

*Hard times.* When all that seems to be left in life is the sadness
and dread, and you feel alone and worthless like one
measly piece of thread.

*But wait,* Is that laughter you hear?
*But wait,* Is that light you see?
Can you feel it? You don't have a fear.
Could it be that the hard times are over?

**Alana Steblecki (13)**
The Sholing Technology College

# Dolphins

D o a flip,
O ver the water you look so big,
L ike a dark shark, you
P ick fish from the sea and
H elp people from the deep blue sea,
I love dolphins because they
N ever hurt people and they
S ave drowning humans.

**Paige Hunt (11)**
The Sholing Technology College

# The Naughty Ones

Into the house they crept
Whilst their owners slept
They'd done this before
To the people next door
Inside the house where they crept.

The flour made the house white
And in the middle of the night
They tore the blinds
And weren't very kind
As they wrecked the whole house in the night.

They came back the very next day
When they thought the owners were away
They were trapped in the house
One owner crept like a mouse
And caught them that very day.

They never did this again
As they caused the owners much pain
They found a new home
And were never alone
As the kittens had children to play with.

**Yasmin Down  (12)**
**The Sholing Technology College**


# Football

Red and white stripes running on the pitch.
They go to tackle, forward into battle.
Fans are screaming loud,
Standing strong and proud.
*Bang!* There goes the ball all the way up the pitch.
Which team's got the ball?
Red and white stripes, of course,
There they are screaming loud.
The ball's in the air and it is now in the net,
We have won the hundred pound bet!

**Ellie Thomas  (14)**
**The Sholing Technology College**

# My Little Sister And Family!

*I want Mummy*
When Play-Doh is hard or dusty,
my sister, she gets very fussy,
she screams and she cries,
she bawls out her eyes,
then wants to cuddle her mummy.

*I want Daddy*
When my sister is wet or muddy,
she gets in a terrible paddy,
her face goes bright red,
she pulls hairs from her head,
then gets a big cuddle from Daddy.

*I want my sister*
When my sister's away, I miss her,
now she's back with a terrible blister,
a small little plaster
on that big disaster,
deserves a big kiss from her sister.

*I love my brother*
My sister, she loves my brother,
she adores him like no other,
and then late at night,
they argue and fight,
but come morning they love one another.

**Sorrel Patrick (12)**
**The Sholing Technology College**


# Spooky Midnight

The moon at midnight has a mysterious glow,
as the witch comes out, you won't know
you're with not a care,
but when she cackles, you'll get a scare!

A shadow passes the window quick,
It's a cat, witch and a flying broomstick!

**Catherine Cove (11)**
**The Sholing Technology College**

# Continuity

*Battle of Hastings*
What exactly happened in 1066?
It all started in a battle at Stamford Bridge.
King Harold heard William the Conqueror was coming to invade,
he needed to stop this French renegade.
Hastings was where the battle begun,
this was a war the Saxons could not have won.
Poor King Harold got shot in the eye,
I felt sorry for that little guy.
For this was the arrow which brought him to his death.
The battle was won within Sir Williams' breath.

*Battle of Iraq*
Alas today in 2004,
this evil world has destruction and war.
Osama bin Laden knocked down the Twin Towers,
when children were at school and people were having their showers.
Many people died that day.
Families were lost, all faces turned grey.
Could it have been ordered by Saddam Hussein?
We already had had a war with him, and now it was to start again.

**Erin Strange  (11)**
**The Sholing Technology College**


# Freedom

Fluffy tails
Floppy ears
Running around
Without any fears.
Playing all day in the sun
Hiding in holes having fun
Sleeping at night
Eating at day
Bunnies can't wait
To come and play.

**Lily Fitzgerald  (11)**
**The Sholing Technology College**

# Covers

You kept me warm when I was cold,
And tucked me in when things went wrong
You snuggled me in when I was scared,
And you were there when no one cared,
You've always been my friend.

You were there when I had no one to cuddle,
And made me feel nice to snuggle,
You were always there when I was alone,
And always there in my home,
We're like two lovers even though you are my covers.

**Emily Bunney  (11)**
**The Sholing Technology College**

# TSTC

The school is great
Silence in the corridors
Teachers always laughing and drinking
College is important

Sholing is great
Home time comes at the end of the day
Oh no! Year 11 will be leaving soon
Look, there is one of my mates . . . see ya!

**Nikki Simpson  (11)**
**The Sholing Technology College**

# My Puppy

Each morning he bounds to my side,
And stares at me with his brown puppy eyes.
I left him for a moment and oh, how he cried,
And each time I leave him, he looks up to ask 'Why?'

**Samantha Mountford  (13)**
**The Sholing Technology College**

# I Feel Invisible!

I wake up in the morning and head downstairs,
I don't care about my looks or the clothes I wear.
I catch a glimpse in the mirror and don't like what I see,
Because, there is a freaky kind of girl looking back at me.

Why should I bother? Why should I care?
Nobody sees me, my life's not fair.

Running down the hall, late for class again,
Drop my books on the floor, look up and then,
Instead of emptiness which I normally see,
There were these deep blue eyes staring down at me.

Why should I bother? Why should I care?
Nobody sees me, my life's not fair.

I am half-asleep,
Walking down the street.
All I can do is stare at my feet,
And it is only the beginning of the week.

Why should I bother? Why should I care?
Nobody sees me, my life's not *fair!*

**Charlotte Parker (13)**
**The Sholing Technology College**

# Friend To Enemy

Friend
Happy, special
Laughing, trusting, reliable,
Shopping, parties, lies, anger,
Enraging, annoying, deceiving,
Hate, fury
Enemy!

**Sadie Partridge (12)**
**The Sholing Technology College**

# Dolphins

Dolphins are cute,
Dolphins are amazing,
Dolphins are smooth,
They love to swim,
They spend all day jumping and leaping about,
They are always happy,
I love them.

Dolphins make great clicking noises,
They don't feel fear,
They know when you like them,
They know when you are near.

*I love them so much!*

**Rachel James  (13)**
**The Sholing Technology College**


# TSTC

The college is excellent
Silence as you walk past the different lessons
Teachers are cool
College rocks

Girls are great
Intelligent, smart and funny
Racing through the corridors
Looking for all the different classrooms
Sholing is excellent!

**Betsy-Ellen King  (11)**
**The Sholing Technology College**

# St Valentine's

Our love is rare, and so satisfying
If I can't have you then I start crying.
The lovely smell of your silky, soft skin,
I always come to you for my deepest sin.

About you the most, I love what's inside,
My love for you is something I can't hide.
You fulfil my dreams, and taste so, so sweet,
The way you make me feel, no one can beat.

You're the one that cheers me when I'm down,
You can make me smile, from what was a frown.
I sit and think about you all day long,
Your soft centre, nothing can go wrong.

I'm sending this letter to let you know,
That on this day, I love chocolate the most.

**Kirby Anderson  (13)**
**The Sholing Technology College**


# Dreams

Clouds floating above my head,
I'm walking on air,
the world around me is flawless, perfect
nothing is going to bring me down from this high,
floating on the clouds of Heaven,
I'm free to feel, to be me,
believe in myself, to live for me,
only I can understand me,
knowing myself like no one will ever know me,
care for yourself as you would care for others,
float up high into the skies
like a field with no boundaries,
dream your dreams.

**Gemma Isaacs  (12)**
**The Sholing Technology College**

# And The Angels Will Fall

Why do angels fall first,
When the world starts to die,
When the happiness ends,
And sorrow comes to reign?

Why do devils survive,
When the Earth starts to crumble,
When the bodies of the damned,
Line the future ahead?

Why does love come second,
To the darkness that grows,
To the suffocating fear
That spreads panic and discord?

Why does hate destroy worlds,
When Hell comes to play,
When screams fill the air
And tears flood the skies?

Why is day fading slowly?
And night getting so much worse?
When the world starts to die,
The angels will fall first.

**Sian Edwards  (12)**
**The Sholing Technology College**


# Love

L oving someone for who they are
O lder, younger, it doesn't matter
V isiting people who make you happy
E verything you have you share.

**Tina Bartlett  (14)**
**The Sholing Technology College**

# The Flame

It started out as just a flame
then it got bigger and a few people came
to watch it burn near a farm.
It started roaring and they raised an alarm.
Some of them rang 999.
They couldn't come quickly enough, they were out of time,
because of the flame.

The noise got louder
buildings turned to powder
but however hard they tried
lots of people cried
because of the fright
of seeing their houses being destroyed in the night
because of the flame

Now it's abandoned, that town,
with no one to be there, no one's around,
to take care of it
and the buildings that were once lit
with fire, are dust in the ground
and no one's around
because of the flame.

**Louisa Cooper (12)**
**The Sholing Technology College**


# Penguins

Waddling along through the thick white snow.
Wind beating down on their wet black skin,
Polar bears are roaring as they go,
But the penguins are determined to win.

Diving like bullets into the deep blue sea,
Swimming along whilst seeking their prey,
To make things worse, the fish start to flee,
After a hard day's work, on the snow they lay.

**Sophie Broyd (12)**
**The Sholing Technology College**

# The Sea

The tide is up,
The fog grows thin,
And all the fish come swimming in.
All is calm,
The night is here,
The seagulls seem to disappear.

The morning comes,
And all has changed,
Then all of a sudden it starts to rain.
The sea gets mad,
Turns murky green,
And flying seaweed can be seen.

The children playing in the sand,
Alarmed to see the red flag turn,
Go rushing home,
Too dangerous here,
Until the green is back in sight,
The sea will be lonely day and night.

The sea is dead,
No waves or current.
Only the occasional splash,
Of a dolphin gone in a dash.
No one plays - it's just no fun,
What has the sea done?

**Ellen Brawley (13)**
**The Sholing Technology College**

# We'll Never Part

*(Dedicated to Sonja)*

*Dear Mum,*

It's over and I miss you so,
But the stars will shine and the moon will glow,
I look upon you and keep you safe,
From all the hurt but you must have faith.

Don't be sad, I'm feeling better,
Well enough to write this letter,
I'm now with all my doggy friends,
Playing around, the fun never ends.

In the clouds I sleep at night,
Wishing you were here, I build up fright,
Missing the hugs, cuddles and kisses
And all those yummy dog food dishes.

It's not bad that I'm not with you anymore,
Touching your face with my paw,
I was ill, you knew I wasn't going to live
But you gave all that you could give.

I see you in the dreams I have,
All the fun that we had,
But just remember I love you,
Because, because I miss you,
So Mummy, Mummy, I'll see you soon!

*Love, Annie.*

**Corinne Seymour  (12)**
**The Sholing Technology College**

# My Valentine Lee

Dear, my one love, luscious lad, Lee Ryan,
All my love I send to you on this day,
I hope you love me as much as I, you,
I hope we will not waste our love away.

Don't forget 'One Love', 'Sorry' and 'Bubblin'
You're my very soul, the love of my life,
I hope that Duncan will soon stop muddlin'
And I hope soon I will become your wife.

You'll never know my true feelings for you,
Roses and red violets are blue, baby,
I will tell you forever 'til I'm blue,
I will grow old with you, one day, maybe?

I want to live my whole life with you, Lee,
All I need to know is how you feel about me.

**Charlotte Prince-Wright (13)**
**The Sholing Technology College**


# My Dog Shadow

Shadow sits on my lap
He can fit through a cat flap
I take him for walks every day
Apart from Sundays.

He has big black eyes and floppy ears
My eyes fill up with tears
With joy and laughter when he plays
With his soft toys on summer days.

He is tan and white
And when he sleeps at night
He is cute as cute can be
For he is my very own puppy.

**Sandra Shotter (12)**
**The Sholing Technology College**

# The Littlest Worm

The littlest worm,
I ever saw,
Got stuck inside
My soda straw.

He said to me,
'Don't take a sip,
Because if you do,
I'll surely slip.'

I took a sip,
And he went down,
Right through my pipes,
He must have drowned.

Now he has gone,
This is the end,
He was my pal,
He was my friend.

**Abbey Charlotte Hennen (14)**
**The Sholing Technology College**


# The Love For Chocolate . . .
# From A Chocoholic

You can spend all day thinking of him,
the one who stole your heart,
but don't let your thoughts lead you astray,
because the next day you're far apart.

But you can spend all year thinking of chocolate,
however, you want it to be,
it can be white, dark or covered in nuts,
but it always tastes lovely to me.

So next time you're lost and don't know what to do,
turn to chocolate, to get you through.

**Juliet Dowrick (13)**
**The Sholing Technology College**

# The Dream

In my world it's quiet and calm,
Nothing coming to any harm.
Everything is perfect and in line,
It could stay like this for all time.

A gentle ripple on the surface of a stream,
It's just so right it's almost a dream.
I lie and let everything go on,
How could my life ever be wrong?

An eagle lands,
The silence is broken.
The dream has stopped,
I have awoken.

Now every day I wonder why,
I stay awake every night.
I feel as though I stand alone,
Waiting for them to come home.

It's now surviving every day that goes past,
Hoping it will be the last.
I want to return to the world I lived in,
But as I now know that will never happen.

I'm now missing something I used to feel and know,
Although my heart did not want to let go.
And now I feel as if I've fallen,
Into the new world and my life has been stolen.

When an eagle landed,
When the silence was broken.
When the dream stopped,
I was woken.

**Hannah Donaldson  (13)**
**The Sholing Technology College**

# My Valentine

Your eyes sparkle like the stars in the sky,
For you I will do anything but die,
You are perfect, you must come from above,
The things I do like about you, I love.

Your red, red lips, incredibly luscious,
Your love to me is very much precious,
This day to me has been one of my best,
Join me forever, my love will not rest.

All sorts of things I want you to shower,
Champagne, chocolate, every kind of flower,
With you I'm having a wonderful time,
Please, please say that you'll be forever mine.

Do you agree that our love is magic?
Never leave me as that would be tragic!

**Katie Mayhew  (13)**
**The Sholing Technology College**


# The Old Willow Tree

The old willow tree,
Standing all on its own,
Sweeps the floor with its long, dangly arms,
Tired of being pushed by the wind.

The old willow tree,
Looks sad and lonely,
Looking for some friends, but no success,
It feels ugly but really it is beautiful.

The old willow tree,
Solemn and old,
Standing elegantly on its legs,
The wind blowing through its leaves. . .

It sounds like it is crying.

**Katherine Hibdige  (13)**
**The Sholing Technology College**

# Behind the Door . . .

Behind the door I saw a ghost,
Floating three feet off the ground.
Behind the door I heard a wolf,
Making a strong, howling sound.
Behind the door I smelt a dead corpse,
Lying so rigid on the floor,
Behind the door I taste a something
Engulfing me whole.
Behind the door I saw a ghost . . .

**Lydia Bloomfield  (11)**
**The Sholing Technology College**


# Summer

S ummer is the hottest season,
U nder the blanket of heat is a town.
M any people have paddling pools,
M any people have fans.
E verybody wears hats to keep cool,
R ain lets the plants grow after this season.

**Danielle Coutts  (13)**
**The Sholing Technology College**


# The Odd Sock

It's small and it's smelly.
It tastes of lime jelly.
It smells of mouldy cheese.
So strong it makes me wheeze.
It's my odd sock!

**Emily Bennett  (11)**
**The Sholing Technology College**

# The Price Of War

The peace has gone
death now sings its song.
Soldiers are ready to fight
the army shows its might.

Bombs are falling
it's so appalling.
Blood is shed
and people lie dead.

War comes at a cost
so many lives are lost.
Babies are crying
as their dads are dying.

**Jenny Allen  (13)**
**The Sholing Technology College**


# Me And My Best Friend

Me and my best friend,
will be together until the end,
she laughs and jokes around a lot,
and yes, she's completely lost the plot!

We've been friends for ages and ages
and we go through all these crazes,
teddies, Barbies - lots and lots of toys,
now it's make-up, clothes and boys.

We go to town all the time
and now I don't know what else rhymes!
But me and my best friend
will be together until the end.

**Jessica King  (14)**
**The Sholing Technology College**

# Monster In The Water!

Lurking in the deep,
Dark, gloomy water,
It makes the children weep,
When you mention the monster in the water.

They flee
From the monster in the water,
And you will soon see
Why you should flee from the water.

Its teeth like swords,
Its eyes are fireballs burning bright.
Its scales, tough as boards,
There goes a child in the night.

Its mouth full of bones,
*Crunch!*
The monster is a no-go zone.
*Crunch!*

**Hazel Atkins  (11)**
**The Sholing Technology College**

# Who Am I?

I am quick
I am fast
I won't last
I am soft and fluffy too
I am so small I fit in a shoe
My ears are long
And whiskers too
I do no wrong
And don't get stuck
Who am I?

*I am a . . . rabbit!*

**Tiffany Bray  (11)**
**The Sholing Technology College**

# Love Not War

Shooting and killing
Shouting and screaming
War is a bloodbath
For religion and greed

Will there ever be peace?
Will there ever be love?
Will there ever be trust?
I don't think so!

Too many chiefs
And not enough Indians
Too many religions
That cause a war

I want harmony and peace
But it will never be
I want love not war
When will it ever be?

**Michaela Brackstone  (13)**
**The Sholing Technology College**


# Tarantulas

Tarantulas are hairy
Spiders are scary
What would you do if they crawled up your back?
Blinding, paralysing, heart-stopping, blast-blinding,
Eating, moving fast.

Tarantulas are big
Spiders are small
Tarantulas could eat liver from a pig
But they don't mind eating anything at all.

**Kirsty Biggs  (13)**
**The Sholing Technology College**

# Do You Love Me?

I never thought there could be someone special
out there for me.

But now I'm all in love because a girl like me
waited patiently for someone to care for me.

Your love is so strong it makes me weak
while it knocks me off my feet.

Now there will be no more crying
then denying.

Now it could be time for me to find out
how first-time love really feels.

You can't carry on playing
there's no time for delaying

Do you love me?

**Katie Linham (12)**
**Wyvern Technology College**


# Yellow

I am the colour yellow,
Bright and lively like the sun.
I am the colour yellow,
Easy going and fun.
And yet I can be subtle,
Quiet, timid and shy,
Like the tiny stars and pale yellow flecks,
That are floating in the sky.
I am the colour yellow,
Bold, strong and tall.
I am the colour yellow,
I can be pale, soft and small.
Like a high-standing sunflower,
That describes me!
And yet I am a buttercup,
Small, but bold and free.

**Aimie Figg (13)**
**Wyvern Technology College**

# Christmas

Hanging up the decorations
Putting up the Christmas tree
Wrapping up all the presents
With a little sparkling tape.

Red and white Christmas hats
Putting the roast turkey on
Hear the pull of Christmas crackers
With the snow falling outside.

Saw Father Christmas last night
On his sleigh
With Rudolph at the front
And others behind.

Having dinner, yum, yum, yum!
Opening presents so much fun
What a shame the day is over,
Say goodbye to Christmas Day,
Christmas will be here again next year

**Laura Hunt  (13)**
**Wyvern Technology College**


# Basketball

Basketball is my favourite sport,
I like the way they dribble up and down the court
I like slam dunk to take me to da hoop,
my favourite play is the alley oop.
I like tricks, flicks and dunks too
let's go one-on-one, me and you.
Up down, round and round,
take it down to the underground,
down there is where we'll play.
We could be taking shots all day.
Walking round the streets in our street cred.
Going home to . . . rest . . . in . . . bed.

**James Hadaway  (13)**
**Wyvern Technology College**

# My Broken Arm

Going home from school I was riding on my bike
Suddenly I was off!
It gave me quite a fright

I got home to my house
My skin was pale and clammy
My brother said, 'It's broken.
No school for you, you're jammy!'

To A&E we went in my mum's car quite quickly
I think that she was worried that I would be feeling sickly
The doctor was an Aussie, she was young and very fit
She sent me for an X-ray, 'Follow the red line, be quick.'

The lady in X-ray moved my arm around
She took some pictures of the bones
My arm began to pound!

They sent me back to see the Aussie, carrying my pics
'There's not much wrong, you've just broken this bone
We can fix that pretty quick
Come with me and sit right down
A cast is what you need
Your bone will mend and that's the end, no more riding
for a few weeks.'

**Adin Vincent (12)**
**Wyvern Technology College**


# Butterflies

As I watch the butterflies
they seem to fly to the sky.

Their wings as colourful as the rainbow
so watch how they glow.

As they fly to the sky
they seem to say . . . 'Bye-bye!'

**Rebecca Hatt (13)**
**Wyvern Technology College**

# Gone To Polish The Moon

'Mama, Mama, where's Papa gone?'
   'He's gone to polish the moon, child,
   He's gone to polish the moon.'

'Why are we leaving Berlin, Mama, why are we leaving Berlin?'
   'We're going away to London, child,
   Our journey will begin.'

'What's a filthy Jew, Mama, am I a filthy Jew?'
   'Someone's fear and pain child,
   You are just a Jew.'

'Why do the bombs come at night, Mama, why do they
                            come at night?'
   'To hide men from the light, child,
   To hide men from the light.'

'Why do you cry in the dark, Mama, why do you cry in the dark?'
   'Daytime tears freeze hearts, child,
   Daytime tears freeze hearts.'

'Mama, Mama, where's Papa gone?'
   'He's gone to polish the moon, child,
   He's gone to polish the moon.'

**Tamsin Cookson (15)**
**Wyvern Technology College**


# The Life In Iraq

In Iraq it was so quiet and still
In Iraq streets started to fill

In Iraq guns and tanks littered the street.
In Iraq the Iraqis and armies meet

In Iraq crying in pain
In Iraq Saddam plays his game.

In Iraq people wonder, *where is the freedom?*
In Iraq people pray for their kingdom.

**Jade Elizabeth Pletts (13)**
**Wyvern Technology College**

# Fair Food

A cow becomes a roast,
Just like a chicken.
I wouldn't like to boast,
But sometimes we might have pork in

A fish gets breaded,
Or sometimes battered,
Or even maybe shredded,
You know, they don't like being flattened.

Apples are cored,
Bananas are sheared,
Although you may be bored,
There is a message to be learnt here.

We eat other living things,
But nothing eats us.
Ah, now your brain has pinged,
Really, I think we should make more fuss!

**Gemma Ralph  (12)**
**Wyvern Technology College**

# All That Is Me

I am the outside, country lanes and steep mountains
I am torrential rain, quick and alive
I am a drink that bubbles and fizzes
and I am a fox, sneaky and sly

I am a beach with great waves for surfing
and sand that is hot to the touch,
I am a phone with the latest technology
and I am a hurricane with speed and gust

I am wellies, not afraid to get muddy
and I am a hawk, can't wait to explore
I am a tele; lots of channels
and I am a tiger not afraid at all

I am the ocean, I am the beach
I am a storm and the sea
I am a whale and I am a monkey,

And that is all that is me.

**Joe Hitchcock  (12)**
**Wyvern Technology College**

# Left To Die . . .

A woman sits with her newborn son,
On a dusty lane,
Her eyes are full of fear and shame,
She's nearly dead but who's to blame?

OK, this woman had lost her way in life,
Made mistakes, did things wrong,
And so her husband left her there,
She was lonely, desperate and needed care,

Then came her son,
A baby boy.
Although she loved her baby son
She knew his life would not be fun.

So she sat there on this dusty street,
Choking, coughing and dying,
Her skin was raw and she felt weak,
She knew her chance of survival was bleak,

She cuddled her baby,
She kissed her son's head,
She whimpered and let out a desperate cry,
But what can you do when you're left to die?

**Emily Goddard (12)**
**Wyvern Technology College**

# My Saturday

It's Saturday morning, it seems quite late
But I look at the clock and it's only eight.
I run downstairs, grab some orange juice and Special K,
This breakfast is the best way to start the day.
Then a quick wash and a brush of my teeth,
'Hurry up,' says Mum, 'it's nearly time.' Good grief!
I brush my hair and put on my kit,
The Solent All Stars. I feel pretty fit.
We jump in the car as it just starts raining
And drive to Fleming Park for the basketball training.
A one-hour session from ten till eleven,
I love basketball, it feels just like Heaven.
Bounce, bounce, bounce, dribble, dribble, dribble,
Pass to a friend, then run to the middle.
The ball's back to me, I turn and I shoot,

*Swish* through the net as the whistle goes hoot.
Back at home it's time for lunch,
Pitta breads, ham and cucumber to munch.
I play with my sister and some of my friends,
When Dad calls us in and playtime ends.
I finish my homework and watch some TV
Before going to bed and falling asleep.

**Amy Tooley (12)**
**Wyvern Technology College**

# Time Is Like A River

Time is like a river,
Only coming once,
Once it's passed by,
It will never come back,

      Time is like a river,
      Only coming once,
      Flowing by secretly,
      Not knowing where it's gone,

            Time is like a river,
            Only coming once,
            All we have are memories
            Of that special piece of time,

      Time is like a river,
      Only coming once,
      Slipping by silently,
      Forgotten by the mind,

Time is like a river,
Only coming once,
There's no getting it back
Once the last drop has gone,

      Time is like a river,
      Only coming once,
      Passing, passing
. . .   . . .   . . .   . . .   . . .   . . . G
                           o
                            n
                             e
                               b
                               y.

**Rachael Lloyd  (12)**
**Wyvern Technology College**

# Who Are The British?

What is British culture?
What do the French think of us?
What food do we eat?
Do we always make a fuss?

We take ideas from Americans,
McDonald's and KFC,
Apparently we're all overweight,
What has British culture done to me?

We drink throughout the day,
All we eat is roast beef.
We're eating up the countryside,
What'll happen to the cows and sheep?

We all moan about the weather,
All it does is rain, rain, rain.
The most famous Brit is David Beckham,
And for everything he does, we all take the blame.

We all play cricket,
Our schools have gone downhill.
Every kid is a yob,
Who will sort it out, who will?

Sort it out everyone,
We're not all like that.
Some people may be . . .

So what is British culture?
Does anyone know these British people?

*Not me!*

**Emily Cooke (12)**
**Wyvern Technology College**

# I Am . . .

I am the colour orange,
Warm, fun and lively.

I am a cloud,
Floating free, wherever I want to be.

I am a pair of old trainers,
Not afraid to get muddy.

I am an autumn tree,
With all the different shades of leaves.

I am a summer breeze,
Gentle, calm and relaxing.

I am a bright red parrot,
Intelligent and amusing.

I am a tropical rainstorm,
Swift, fast and unpredictable.

I am an old, withered tree,
But best of all,

*I am me!*

**Tom Curran  (12)**
**Wyvern Technology College**

# If Life Was . . .

If life was a bouquet of flowers,
A day would be a petal.
If life was a building,
A day would be a room.
If life was the sky,
A day would be a bird.
If life was a mountain,
A day would be a rock.

If life was night,
A day would be a star.
If life was acres of fields,
A day would be a crop.
If life was a country,
A day would be a village.
If life was a rainforest,
A day would be an insect.

If life was war,
A day would be a gun.

**Hayley Cumner  (13)**
**Wyvern Technology College**

# My Brother, A Hero

My brother came back,
Black and blue,
He wouldn't say why,
But I knew.

My brother is a hero,
He fights lions in their dens
He climbs the highest mountains,
And is back by ten.

My brother is a hero,
He puts out fires, fires that blaze,
But he's so modest,
He won't accept our praise.

My brother is a hero,
He rescues those afar,
He doesn't talk about it,
But I know he's a star.

My brother is a hero,
He saves some drowning kids,
Then stops off for a drink,
At his best friend Sid's.

My brother is a hero,
He fights for people's rights,
He never seems to lose,
And is never out at nights.

My brother is a hero,
He saves me when I'm down,
I don't know what I'd do,
If he was not around.

My brother is a hero,
My hero, just mine!

**Bethan Evans  (12)**
**Wyvern Technology College**

# Hallowe'en

Lights in our pumpkins
Shine in
The dark.
Woods they are scary,
Dogs
They do bark
Children are off
                    quick
                        down
                            the
                                street

*Knocking!*
On doors
*Shouting*
'Trick or treat?'
It is October now
Hallowe'en
Witches on broomsticks
Ghosts can be seen.
Owls they do hoot,
Bats they do fly
Night
Is so
Scary
My friends and I
See stars a-twinkling
Up in the sky
Light our way home
Back to our mum
*Had* a good night
Had lots of
Fun.

**Louise Jones (12)**
**Wyvern Technology College**

# Africa

The night falls asleep
While the sun wakes up
People drinking water out of their clay cups
Preparing for the day ahead
Getting the children out of bed
Going to collect the crops
Before the harvest season stops.

Trying to gather a bit of money
They'll be lucky if they afford bread and honey
Working all day without a stop
They need food but there are no shops.

They pray for a better life
Without any struggle or strife
The night wakes up
While the sun falls asleep
And while the darkness closes in
The African people weep.

**Mark Dawkins  (12)**
**Wyvern Technology College**

# Seasons Poem

Spring is the season when all things come to life,
Spring is when trees put on their clothes,
Spring is when things turn green,
Spring is kind, winter is mean.

Summer is my favourite, it is the best,
It is where people go out to play,
Summer is hot, the sun shines down,
It is great, it doesn't make me frown.

Autumn is when greens turn to brown,
Autumn is falling leaves every day,
Sticks and conkers, fir cones and acorns,
Come falling down covering front lawns.

Winter is cold, Jack Frost is coming,
Winter is freezing, icy and snowy,
Winter is the season of short days,
This is when Jack Frost comes out and plays.

**Matt Burrows  (12)**
**Wyvern Technology College**

# Someone To Love

When I was younger, I wanted a pet
Now I'm a vet.

When he was younger he wanted money
Now he is a lawyer

When I was an adult I wanted a house
And it's a joy to me now

All these things made me happy
Except one thing

All I wanted as I grew
Was a family . . .
I didn't get that!

Maybe you've guessed
I was an orphan child

No one to love me
Can someone . . .
*Please!*

**Louisa Monckton  (12)**
**Wyvern Technology College**

# Arthur's Widow

From the walls of this castle
A great battle was seen
On midsummer's day in 1314,
Men in white dresses
    Hallowed
        Ground.
A misty gathering;

A *grassy* mound.

Behold the beauty
    Of the
        Rising sun.
Where Arthur's widow
      Became
        A
          Nun.
A prison of bad,
      A fortress,
         A keep,
Voices
    And
      Elizabeth
        Weeps.

**Jessica Harrison  (13)**
**Wyvern Technology College**

# Old Man's Footsteps

He walks at night,
when the sky is clear
and the air is cool.

He walks at night,
along the beach
when the area's calm
and the ocean's sleeping.

He walks at night,
through fields
and over hills
listening to the cool breeze
whistling through the trees.

He walks at night,
past our houses
through the village
the only sound you can hear
is his footsteps on the ground

He walks at night,
when nobody is there
the only thing you can see
are the footprint he has left
like a trail as he walks
on his journey through
the village

He walks at night,
every night,
until eventually
all of his footprints
fade away . . .

**Josh Calder  (12)**
**Wyvern Technology College**

# My Day

Waking up at 8am,
My hair all frizzy and fat,
Trying to find my riding gear
My boots, my gloves, my hat.

I run downstairs in a flash
Some toast is all I eat,
Before I'm ready, it's time to go
With no boots upon my feet.

I get in the car, it's to the farm
The horse is still asleep,
We have to brush his mane and tail
And still clean out his feet.

We tack him up for a ride
In the schooling ring,
We do trotting and dressage
Even galloping.

Back home again, in time for lunch
But I also need a wash,
Going shopping later on
To spend lots of dosh.

Tops, trousers, belts and shoes
Tammy and New Look,
But I can't resist the new 'Hartland'
My all time favourite book

Later on it's time for tea
To Pizza Hut we go,
Ice cream factory is on the list
But Mum and Dad say, 'No!'

It's the end of my day,
With memories to keep,
I close my eyes slowly
And dream myself to sleep.

**Hannah Lyons (12)**
**Wyvern Technology College**

# From Mum To Me

*(Thinking of Richard always, sent to Iraq, 11th October)*

I 'm here now Mum.
>    I don't like it Mum.

R etribution
>    Everywhere
>>        Mum

>    Rebels storming the streets

A live human being smuggled from his day job

>    Aeroplanes tear through the sky

Q uestions
>    Everywhere
>>        Mum

>    Queries, how? Who? What? Why?

**Thomas Jacobs  (12)**
**Wyvern Technology College**


# It's Just Not Much Fun Anymore

It's just not much fun anymore,
I smell a familiar smell, but it doesn't belong to anyone,
I look at our den, it's deathly silent and overgrown with weeds,
I look at the flower beds we used to trample on, they're neat.

It's just not much fun anymore,
I look at the playground we played in, it's deserted,
I picture our school football team's shirt - your number will never
>>>>        be worn again,
I stare at the empty chair, wishing it were filled.

It's just not much fun anymore,
Our class photo, your face is missing,
There would always be something to talk about when you were here,
I try to find a memory of you, but I simply can't.

*It's just not much fun anymore!*

**Hannah Soley  (12)**
**Wyvern Technology College**

# The Figure In Grey

I once saw a figure standing all alone,
A shadow-grey cloak hung over his shoulders covering jagged bone,
I saw him turn his head to me and felt his deathly gaze,
And in those eyes I saw his memory through a misty haze.

I saw as Alexander stormed through mighty Persia,
I saw as all his men bought glory through foreign murder,
I saw as Julius Caesar conquered for his gold,
And poets saw and glorified and bloody tale told.

Now I watched as time sped by to almost the modern day,
And a smile passed over the face of the stony figure in grey,
Men dreamed up new machines and invented lethal arms,
Expanding their ability to cause fellow humans harm.

I watched as war followed war and countless numbers died,
I despaired as I watched as so many could not hide,
They could not hide or shelter find, so many tried to run,
But it seemed that no one could escape from those bullets
and those guns.

And then the Great War ravaged the world and shocked I could see,
Just how much human blood was spilt in the quest for victory,
Then the Second War came, just as hellish as before,
And oh so many perished in this horrific war.

But I saw that the figure's cloak was not black but grey,
Because the human heart between good and evil does often
tend to sway,
For Man is not truly war-like; he really wants to help,
And whether his goodness will prevail only time will tell.

I then asked the figure in grey who he really was,
And he replied, 'I'm an onlooker watching something that is lost,
But sooner or later it will find its way - there is meaning in
what you saw.'
And suddenly I realised who he was: the figure in grey was War.

**Ben Harris  (12)**
**Wyvern Technology College**

# Dying Fairy Tale

It walks
in and out
of people's lives
feeling just like a
fairy tale
too good
to be true

It's as if
it will never end,
but it does
then
all of a sudden
rain surrounds you
creating an ocean
but you can't drown
because
you already have

And then you're
dragged
swept
pulled
to shore
the water's gone
and you're back again
with bright sunshine
and a door
the end
of a painful heartache
is the beginning
of the fairy tale
all over again
but this time
for real.

**Jessica Hanford (12)**
**Wyvern Technology College**

# I'm Robo

I'm Robo 129,
Freshly off the building line.
I'm brand new and I shine,
I'm brand new and feeling fine.

Twisting, turning,
Blowtorch is burning.
Screeching, scratching,
Welding, patching.

I'm Robo 318,
Always on time and never late.
I've got no brain, got no heart,
I was put together part by part.

Buzzing, clicking,
The clock is ticking.
Shouting, screaming,
Shining gleaming.

I'm Robo 771,
So many jobs, no time to have fun.
Work, work, work, no time to rest,
I've got no heart inside my chest.

I've got a square head,
I'm not alive, I'm not dead.
I have no human voice,
I wish I was human but I've no choice.

I'm Robo 645.
I run on battery, I'm not alive.
My brain is a microchip,
I don't sleep, I don't kip.

I'm metal, no skin,
No blood, just tin.
No brain, no heart,
I am state of the art.

**Alex Scurlock (13)**
**Wyvern Technology College**

# Celebrations

On my birthday,
the dog ate the cake,
Dad went mad,
and the presents did break.

At Christmas,
Mum went crazy,
the turkey got burned,
so did the gravy.

On Nan's anniversary,
the cat was sick on the food,
Mum shouted at my brother,
he got in a mood.

Why do people say,
celebrations are fun?
Almost everyone's angry,
we're not happy 'til they're done.

But I suppose it's a holiday,
and we get the day off,
all we do these days,
is eat and scoff.

Cakes and biscuits are the best,
we all deserve a well-earned rest,
because we see family and friends!

**Kealey Rigden  (12)**
**Wyvern Technology College**

# She Was Gone

Some say she walks alone
some say she walks on by
people see her disappear
her soul goes to the sky.

She floats along like a single cloud
her mind filled with many things
the words all spill away
but she's still attached with strings.

Some say she lives in hate
and that she wants to die
some say she hurts with trying
and falls and starts to cry.

The truth may be found out
about her secret fear
she's scared what friends will say
and what she fears to hear.

Some say she gets troubled
and walks alone in the hall
her body feels frail and weak
behind her own brick wall.

Then one day she lost all hope
and felt like she was wrong
soon she withered and started to fade
and her inner self was gone.

**Tesni Winfield (12)**
**Wyvern Technology College**

# The Dark Shadow Of War

It's wartime again, the sounds of guns firing and missiles
Thundering through the sky flood into my mind.
As I look out of my bedroom window, as I weep and I cry, I remember.

As though I'm going back in time,
I remember the dark shadow that cast itself over my beloved home,
The day we found out that Father had died.

It changed my life.
I gazed as my mother fell to the hospital floor, as if she, too,
Had dropped dead,
She didn't move, she just lay there in silence.

I just stood there as a tear trickled down my pale cheek
And fell to the ground,
That was the day the dark shadow came,
It hasn't left since.

The next day, after my father's death,
I came home from school, to see
My home explode into a pile of ashes.

A nurse came up to me and said that Mother was in a critical state,
And a few days later, she died,
I ended up in a foster home.

That is why at the crippled aged of 83,
I don't want my children going through their parents' death, like I did.

So I have decided to leave this world, and family, and give up.

**Vicky Bacon  (12)**
**Wyvern Technology College**

# James The Name-Caller

There was a boy whose name was James,
Who kept on calling people names,
All day he sat upon his chair,
Thinking of names to cause despair.

When he finally thought of a name,
He started to play his unfriendly game,
He then stood up from his chair,
And crept up behind his classmate Claire.

He whispered in her delicate ear,
The words she wouldn't like to hear,
'Claire, you are a disgrace,
I cannot stand the sight of your face!'

His words he chose as an aim to try,
To make his next poor victim cry,
But as she turned, after a while,
Instead of tears there came a smile.

For on James' face, oozing spots appeared,
And from his chin there grew a beard.
She said with evil in her eyes,
'You clearly have not seen through my disguise,
For although I wear a little girl's dress,
I am, in fact, the powerful sorceress!

So take your words and nasty lies,
And into a mirror cast your eyes,
For upon your face I've played a trick,
One that will make others feel quite sick.'

James rushed to the mirror in the loo,
Took one look and said, 'Oh poo!'
The beard and spots he found quite shocking,
'I guess this means an end to my mocking!'

The moral of this story goes,
If you're mean, it really shows!

**James McCowan (11)**
**Wyvern Technology College**

# My Saturday

I wake up early, I love my bed,
What to do in the day ahead?
On with the TV, it's Dick and Dom!
Why the hell did I turn it on?

It's time to work maths and tech,
Get it done or get it in the neck!
Sums and writing, work and drawing,
All this work is so, so boring!

That work was hard, I need some food,
No more work, I'm not in the mood.
Beans on toast is all I eat,
I watch TV and rest my feet.

TV, TV, all afternoon,
Believe it or not it's dinner soon!
After that is more TV,
Then I go to bed and watch a *DVD!*

**George James  (12)**
**Wyvern Technology College**

# What Is Art?

If I were a view, I would be an 'Ikea' sign,
at first glance, a rusty monstrosity,
both dilapidated and decrepit.
always complained about at council meetings,
but eventually people would give up and let me be

And when they did,
they might think that maybe I am not that bad
not so strange,
a work of art,
a masterpiece of character,

I am a masterpiece of character,
not much to look at,
not much to get excited about,
to scream and shout about,
but really nice on the inside,
like a sour gobstopper with a sweet strawberry inside.

**Katie McBain  (12)**
**Wyvern Technology College**